following jesus every day

GOSP
MEDITAT
FOR
DAILY LIVING

ALAN J. HOMMERDING

following jesus every day

GOSPEL
MEDITATIONS
FOR
DAILY LIVING

ALAN J. HOMMERDING

*For Ann Celeen Dohms,
faithful follower of the Lord*

FOLLOWING JESUS EVERY DAY
Gospel Meditations for Daily Living

Author: Alan J. Hommerding
Editor: Michael E. Novak
Production Editor/Copy Editor: Marcia T. Lucey
Cover and Book Design: Chris Broquet
Director of Publications: Mary Beth Kunde-Anderson
Production Manager: Deb Johnston

Following Jesus Every Day: Gospel Meditations for Daily Living, Copyright © 2012, World Library Publications, the music and liturgy division of J. S. Paluch Company, Inc., 3708 River Road, Suite 400, Franklin Park, Illinois 60131-2158. 800 566-6150 wlpmusic.com

Scripture excerpts taken from the *New Revised Standard Version* of the Bible, Copyright © 1989, Division of Christian Education of the National Council of the Churches of Christ in the USA. Used by permission. All rights reserved.

WLP 001758
ISBN 978-1-58459-592-2

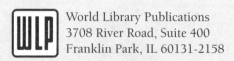

World Library Publications
3708 River Road, Suite 400
Franklin Park, IL 60131-2158

introduction

When I was in the fifth grade, one of the first chapters in the book for our religion class focused on the cross. Our assignment was to write an essay about Jesus' death on the cross. As part of my essay, I included quotations from the Passions of Matthew, Mark, Luke, and John, stories that had affected me greatly when I'd heard them in church during Holy Week. When December rolled around, we were given an end-of-semester opportunity for extra credit. I decided to do the same exercise with the Christmas stories from Matthew, Mark, Luke, and John. In alarm, I told the teacher that our classroom's Bibles were *missing* Mark and John's Christmas stories! Not only that, but Matthew and Luke were almost completely different—we obviously needed to replace our Bibles with correct ones!

I was sent to the pastor to have my concerns addressed. Luckily, he was able to explain gently to me that the Gospels aren't written like newspapers, merely recounting things that had happened to Jesus, but they are four different ways to get to know Jesus. He also was able to guide me into understanding that it had been the earlier assignment that semester—the passion, death, and resurrection of Jesus—that was truly at the heart of the Christian faith and that it was, in that way, the real starting point of the gospel story.

So, like any other fifth grader, I decided to read all four Gospels straight through during Christmas vacation and then—the following year—the entire Bible. That exercise generated many more questions—and many more visits with the pastor! (Incidentally, if you read five chapters of the Bible each day, you can get through the whole Bible in a calendar year; I did the math.)

I don't tell this story to illustrate what sort of child scriptural savant I was, but rather to share how fortunate I was to be encouraged at that time to get to know Jesus better by a deeper exploration of the Gospels, and of the Bible as a whole. That experience has stayed with me throughout the years as I continue to cycle through the three years of the Roman Catholic *Lectionary for Mass*, re-read the whole Bible, and teach scripture occasionally along the way. These experiences were also responsible for this book's predecessor, *Everyday Psalms*.

Like *Everyday Psalms,* this book began as a spiritual discipline for the great ninety days of the Lent and Easter seasons. Fortunately, there are just fewer than ninety total chapters in the four Gospels, which led to the "chapter a day" approach in which I selected one verse from the chapter (not an easy task—there's a *lot* packed into each chapter!), reflected on the verse for a bit, assigned myself one task for the day that would reinforce the lesson of that verse, and said a brief discipleship prayer. As with *Everyday Psalms,* I gravitated toward verses that are not present in the Roman Catholic *Lectionary for Mass,* or verses from familiar narratives that, in my experience, tend to get overlooked or ignored in scriptural commentaries or preaching.

As these meditations moved from a personal spiritual journal to more concrete form, I wanted to explore further how the life and ministry of Jesus in the Gospels was related to the life and ministry of Israel's prophets. Christians usually think of Jesus as being the fulfillment of the prophets—and he certainly is—but since my journey was focused on discipleship, it became clearer and clearer to me how much Jesus and the evangelists were heirs, perhaps even disciples, of Israel's prophets. I followed the architectural tradition (perhaps its best known example is in the cathedral at Chartres) of the evangelists standing on the shoulders of Israel's four major prophets. Both the public ministry of Jesus and the evangelists' portrayals of it owe much of their vision to the heritage of the prophets.

Rather than read each Gospel straight through (as I did in grade school, and have done a number of times since then), I took a different approach this time, reading across the chapters of each: I would read the first chapter of each of the four Gospels, then the second chapters, and so on. This gave me an interesting additional perspective, as the different structures of the Gospels and their varying lengths led to unexpected convergences and divergences in the telling of the story. Since I began this exercise on Ash Wednesday, this also meant that I was reading the Passion narratives in the middle of the Easter season, another way to reflect on the profound relationship between the Passion and the Resurrection. I also received the blessing of ending with Matthew's farewell scene on Pentecost Sunday.

While it was not my intent to make a separation between the Jesus of history and the Christ of faith, I did find myself most often referring to Jesus by that name. It is the name that his family, friends, and followers used and knew him by as they tried to come to understand, day by day, what it means to know him and to be a disciple of his, and how the reign of God was being revealed to them through his life and ministry. In some places I do refer to Jesus and God, or Christ and God. This is not any sort of denial of Jesus' divinity or place in the Trinity, but emerges from a way that the evangelists and Saint Paul themselves use this sort of vocabulary.

Like all of us, I continue to walk my imperfect, stumbling way of discipleship, striving to follow the Lord Jesus as best I can. Reflecting on the Gospels in the manner presented in this book has deepened my awareness of the call to and demands of discipleship. I've come to know that the life of faith and all of life is enriched and empowered by growing in the grace of Jesus Christ through the Gospels of Matthew, Mark, Luke, and John.

Alan Hommerding
Pentecost Sunday 2010

FOLLOWING JESUS WITH MATTHEW
JESUS THE TEACHER

Often referred to as the "Jewish" Gospel, Matthew quite frequently places Yeshua bar Yussef *(Jesus, the son of Joseph, as he would have been known) in the role of Rabbi/Teacher. The Jewish heritage of Jesus can lead us to know our own rich legacy from Judaism. Jesus as Rabbi or Teacher calls us back to the dynamic, intimate relationship we must have with God, as he instructs, guides, challenges, affirms, and "schools" us in discipleship. Then we can also be named and known as "_____ bat Yeshua" or "_____ bar Yeshua"—a true disciple who is daughter or son of Jesus.*

PRAYER

Teach me, O Lord,
to honor the rich heritage of my faith;
teach me, O Lord,
so that I may show others the way of your
Spirit and truth.

LIVING THE PRAYER

Today I will make a dedicated effort to be a guide or teacher for someone seeking to follow Jesus.
In what ways, even seemingly small ones, can I be a "teacher" for another Christian? Could this happen in an unexpected way or an unusual place or time? Who do I not think of as a teacher, to my own detriment?

THE GOSPEL VISION OF THE PROPHETS

The Lord God has given me
    the tongue of a teacher,
that I may know how to sustain
    the weary with a word.
Morning by morning he wakens—
    wakens my ear
    to listen as those who are taught.
(Isaiah 50:4)

MATTHEW 1:5

. . . and Salmon the father of Boaz by Rahab.

*"God is in the details," the saying goes. This genealogical
mention of Rahab—a Gentile prostitute (see Joshua 2)—in Jesus'
ancestry is precisely such a God-filled detail. She is not such an
odd ancestor for him who spent much of his time proclaiming the
reign of God to all kind of "outsiders," including prostitutes. The
whole story of Christian scripture is made up of those who seemed
atypical for God's great spiritual work: a peasant couple from a
little town, their son who was killed like a common criminal, the
unemployed fishermen huddled afraid in an upper room. Nobody is
too weak or odd or unexpected to be an essential part of God's plan.*

PRAYER

You call us each by name, O God.
When I think I am too lowly,
unlikely to make a difference,
help me know that your grace
is what makes me your chosen servant.

LIVING THE PRAYER

*Today I will reconsider someone I thought could not be a follower
of Christ.*
Do I make quick, too-frequent judgments about who can
and cannot be a disciple? Are these judgments based on my
own biases, fears, or prejudices? Do I make these judgments
about myself?

THE GOSPEL VISION OF THE PROPHETS

For I will pour water on the thirsty land,
    and streams on the dry ground;
I will pour my spirit upon your descendants,
    and my blessing on your offspring.
(Isaiah 44:3)

MATTHEW 2:22

And after being warned in a dream, Joseph went away to the district of Galilee.

Bible scholars often point out the five-fold division of Matthew's Gospel, imitating the five books of the Torah. Less attention is paid to the way the story of Jesus' birth involves five dreams (Joseph has four, the magi have one). These dreams (or visions) are important as the work of God's spirit and a source of prophecy (another inheritance from the Hebrew scriptures), a way to discern the will of God or the voice of God speaking, sometimes through angel messengers. Living out God's will, as we read in all five dream accounts, takes courage, dedication, and real love for the people and the mission God has placed in our care.

PRAYER

Keep me confident
in your sustaining power, Lord.
Refresh and strengthen me
so I may face each day renewed by your love,
and act according to your will.

LIVING THE PRAYER

Today I will listen carefully for the voice of God and God's messengers.
Who are the angel messengers of God speaking in my life today? Do I fail to listen because I fear the way their message will call upon me to change my life?

THE GOSPEL VISION OF THE PROPHETS

I will pour out my spirit on all flesh;
    your sons and your daughters shall prophesy,
your old men shall dream dreams,
    and your young men shall see visions.
(Joel 2:28)

MATTHEW 4:1

Then Jesus was led up by the Spirit into the wilderness to be tempted by the devil.

Matthew, Mark, and Luke all agree that the Spirit of Jesus' baptism caused him to go to the desert. But they give different modes: in Mark the Spirit drives Jesus; in Luke he goes because he is filled with the Spirit. In Matthew, the Spirit of his baptism leads Jesus, so Jesus becomes a disciple of the Spirit. It might seem odd, after the glories of the baptismal scene, for the Spirit to lead Jesus off on his own to face Satan, facing his human nature in desert dryness as he had faced it in the Jordan's waters. But in that blazing crucible, Jesus reinforces what he would show on Calvary: it is through his steadfast, humble obedience that he would conquer Satan.

PRAYER

Send your Spirit upon me today
as you did at my baptism, O Lord.
Let me be led, not by temptation,
but by your Spirit within me.

LIVING THE PRAYER

Today I will discern how the Spirit is active in my life.
How does the Spirit act in my life? How has the Spirit acted in the past: leading me, driving me, filling me? Am I open to all these different actions of the Spirit?

THE GOSPEL VISION OF THE PROPHETS

Not by might, nor by power, but by my spirit,
says the LORD of hosts.
(Zechariah 4:6)

MATTHEW 5:37

"Let your word be 'Yes, Yes' or 'No, No'; anything more than this comes from the evil one."

One might wonder what Jesus would make of the many books (including this one) explaining or interpreting what seems to be, to him, a very direct and clear "Yes or No" message. This chapter of Matthew (better known as the Sermon on the Mount) contains some of the most often-quoted teaching from Jesus; in it Matthew distills some of Jesus' most essential wisdom. His "Yes/ No" directive provides us with an excellent lens through which to view the Sermon's—and all of Jesus'—teachings. It also gives us a way to "interpret" his teaching in our everyday living, the most important commentary on the Gospel we will ever create.

PRAYER

You know my heart, O Lord,
and you know when my lips
do not speak its truth;
give me courage to proclaim
the Good News of Christ
clearly and boldly.

LIVING THE PRAYER

Today I will speak forthrightly and clearly.
How many times have I hesitated to speak or live clearly, even when I knew a simple "Yes" or "No" was the right answer? How can I speak the truth without lapsing into the self-righteousness Jesus detested?

THE GOSPEL VISION OF THE PROPHETS

They all deceive their neighbors,
    and no one speaks the truth;
they have taught their tongues to speak lies;
    they commit iniquity and are too weary to repent.
(Jeremiah 9:5)

MATTHEW 6:6

"But whenever you pray, go into your room and shut the door and pray to your Father who is in secret; and your Father who sees in secret will reward you."

It could seem that Jesus is saying that we should never pray with others or pray in public. Since Jesus did both those things, this certainly isn't his point. He is warning—as he so often does— against hypocrisy or self-righteousness. For those who prayed publicly for the sole purpose of being seen and admired as pray-ers, Jesus says being seen and admired by others will be their entire reward. Whether we pray publicly or privately, whether as a leader of prayer or a member of the faithful assembly, the sole purpose of our praying must be the praise and honor of God.

PRAYER

I call to you, I come to you, Mighty God.
Hear and answer my prayers
offered with a sincere heart.
Seeking to do your will is my reward.

LIVING THE PRAYER

Today I will scrutinize my motivations for praying.
Why do I pray? Is it to seek God genuinely? If I lead prayer in public, how do I direct attention away from me and toward God?

THE GOSPEL VISION OF THE PROPHETS

These people draw near with their mouths
    and honor me with their lips,
    while their hearts are far from me,
and their worship of me is a human
commandment learned by rote.
(Isaiah 29:13)

MATTHEW 7:15

"Beware of false prophets, who come to you in sheep's clothing but inwardly are ravenous wolves."

We can speculate whether or not Jesus' listeners knew Aesop's fable of the wolf in sheep's clothing (Aesop lived seven hundred years earlier). Of more interest to us as disciples is this teaching from Jesus, who—five chapters later—will tell his followers to be wise as serpents but innocent as doves, since he is sending them out as sheep into the midst of wolves. Who could blame his followers if they were to get confused with all this animal imagery? We, his followers today, have to step back and recognize Jesus' total understanding of how the "real" world works and the attributes that a true disciple, not a false prophet, will have. We have nowhere else to look for our example but to Jesus himself.

PRAYER

Shelter me, O Lord,
keep me safe, protect me.
Let me always rejoice in you,
my refuge.

LIVING THE PRAYER

Today I will allow the Lord to be my refuge.
Can I spare a few moments to think about what I may need to be sheltered from? Is one of them the busy-ness that doesn't allow "a few moments"? How can God be my shelter? How will I rejoice?

THE GOSPEL VISION OF THE PROPHETS

Those who are wise understand these things;
     those who are discerning know them.
For the ways of the LORD are right,
     and the upright walk in them,
     but transgressors stumble in them.
(Hosea 14:9)

MATTHEW 8:11

"I tell you, many will come from east and west and will eat with Abraham and Isaac and Jacob in the kingdom of heaven."

Much of Israel's history was divided between northern and southern kingdoms, not unlike the United States. There was much contentiousness about which one of them God favored. Jesus adds insult to injury here by saying that God's preference will not be for one part of Israel or another, but for nations lying outside of it, symbolized here by east and west. Israel's patriarchs will also prefer to extend the biblical sign of welcome and unity—the shared meal table—to those outside Israel who have faith and live righteously. Much of the divisiveness, presumptuousness, and self-righteousness that Jesus encountered is still around today. So is his startling prediction. Will we be surprised by who's at that table?

PRAYER

How wide is your embrace,
loving God!
May my life manifest,
here and now,
the boundless span
of your heavenly banquet.

LIVING THE PRAYER

Today I will open my eyes to see those outside my own "kingdom" of choice.

What boundaries do I set up in my life? Do I work to preserve them, even though they limit my discipleship?

THE GOSPEL VISION OF THE PROPHETS

For from the rising of the sun to its setting my name is great among the nations, and in every place incense is offered to my name, and a pure offering; for my name is great among the nations, says the LORD of hosts.
(Malachi 1:11)

MATTHEW 9:37

Then Jesus said to his disciples, "The harvest is plentiful, but the laborers are few."

Farming is relentless work. Soil and seed need constant tending, weather is fickle. Moreover, when crops are ready, they are ready NOW. They will rot, wither, or be eaten by creatures of the field if not harvested promptly. For a farmer to have a bountiful harvest and not enough laborers is a dilemma, one that not only wastes the crop, but can prove to be life-threatening down the road. In our world of fast food and 24-hour supermarkets, we lose sight of the dire urgency that Jesus' disciples would have heard in this warning. How sad—perhaps sinful—to be blessed by God with this bounty, only to have it wasted for lack of help. The yield is still plentiful today. Ready, laborers?

PRAYER

Lord of the harvest,
send me out, a laborer
ready to work for you
in my daily living.
Send me to help reap the bounty
of your love, mercy, justice,
joy, grace, peace, and salvation.

LIVING THE PRAYER

Today I will stop being lazy and work to bring in the harvest of faith.
What person or situation in my life is ready to be gathered in for God? Do I always assume that someone else will tend to this if I don't? What "famine" might this cause later on?

THE GOSPEL VISION OF THE PROPHETS

The harvest is past, the summer is ended,
and we are not saved.
(Jeremiah 8:20)

"Whatever town or village you enter, find out who in it is worthy, and stay there until you leave."

Before the gospel message can be received, gospel messengers must be received. As Jesus is giving his instructions for mission, it is easy to imagine some disciples wishing he'd backtrack and explain exactly how to determine who is "worthy" to be a host household. Someone who already knows the gospel? A place where they put a good supper on the table? Given Jesus' tendency to upset expectations, it could very well be a household that's exactly the opposite! It would have been easier for the disciples, and definitely easier for us, if Jesus had laid out explicit methods and guidelines for finding this "worthy" place. But this points out how much cooperation and creativity is expected of us in the mission of proclaiming the Good News.

PRAYER

Help, Lord?
I truly want to
discover places where
your good news of salvation
can be received.
Grant me a clear vision
and the Spirit's inspiration
for your mission.

LIVING THE PRAYER

Today I will find a "worthy" recipient for the gospel.
How do I exercise my responsibility for finding new places to give witness to the gospel? Do I go only places where I am guaranteed easy success?

THE GOSPEL VISION OF THE PROPHETS

The LORD said to me: Mortal, all my words that I shall speak to you receive in your heart and hear with your ears.
(Ezekiel 3:10)

MATTHEW 11:30

"For my yoke is easy, and my burden is light."

This passage needs to be reflected upon deeply before we accuse Jesus of false advertising. A lazy spirituality can mistakenly presume that following Jesus means no burdens, no yoke. But this isn't what he's promising. In agrarian societies, yoking beasts of burden together lightened the load for the beasts and improved the work of the people involved as well. When we share our daily discipleship—whatever it may be—fully with Jesus, it makes the work easier than going it alone, and lightens the burden. This is why the whole teaching of this passage begins with Jesus saying, "Come unto me." As we strive to fulfill the command to love God and neighbor completely—not an easy or light task—we go first to Jesus.

PRAYER

When I am sluggish in spirit
and do not want to deal with
the burdens of life,
may I come to you, living God,
to find in you the energy and strength
for the undertakings you give me.

LIVING THE PRAYER

Today I will ease one of my burdens by sharing it with Jesus.
As a disciple, am I a "do-it-yourself" type? How does failing to share the gospel mission with Jesus limit other aspects of following him?

THE GOSPEL VISION OF THE PROPHETS

For the yoke of their burden,
    and the bar across their shoulders,
    the rod of their oppressor,
    you have broken as on the day of Midian.
(Isaiah 9:4)

MATTHEW 12:8

"For the Son of Man is lord of the sabbath."

There is a recurring tension in the Judeo-Christian tradition between ritualized, formal worship and the doing of what is right and good in the world. In the teaching of the two great commands—loving God and loving neighbor—Jesus shows us that it is best to live in a both/and world, one in which we set aside time for worship of God, worship that lead us to live a life that is righteous. But the complex and rigorous codes that humans tend to set up to promote worship sometimes get in the way of that righteous life, and we have to make the either/or choice. When our human limitations don't allow the both/and, Jesus makes it clear: God is in the good we do.

PRAYER

I bless you, my God!
My worship belongs to you alone.
Bless me, too:
let me live a just life,
one that is truly
a sacrifice of praise
to your honor and glory.

LIVING THE PRAYER

Today I will reflect on how my worship is a "good deed" and my good deeds are worship.
Do I ever excuse myself from observing the Lord's Day because I've been "good" during the week? Have there been times that my religious observance kept me from acting righteously?

THE GOSPEL VISION OF THE PROPHETS

For I desire steadfast love and not sacrifice,
    the knowledge of God rather than burnt offerings.
(Hosea 6:6)

MATTHEW 13:3

And Jesus told them many things in parables, saying: "Listen! A sower went out to sow."

The next verse could be "and he wasn't very good at his job, since the seed went everywhere!" God, the sower, seems to be sloppy; you'd think the divine hand would be more precise. But this is how abundant and generous the hand of God is. Some gets flung on the road, some gets eaten by birds, some lands on useless rock, some flies into the weeds . . . so what? To our limited view, this seems careless, even reckless. But God will not risk a missed opportunity for divine wisdom to take hold. For our part, we must be sure that our lives are the fertile place where that seed can fall, help us die to ourselves, to yield an abundant harvest.

PRAYER

How wonderful your word,
God of wisdom!
How extravagantly
you spread it everywhere!
Help me to be open,
ready to receive it, grow in its grace,
producing a rich harvest for you.

LIVING THE PRAYER

Today I will clear the weeds from my ears, the rocks from my heart. Do I have "selective hearing" for God's word? Have I seen that word grow in places I doubted it would?

THE GOSPEL VISION OF THE PROPHETS

So shall my word be that goes out from my mouth;
    it shall not return to me empty,
but it shall accomplish that which I purpose,
    and succeed in the thing for which I sent it.
(Isaiah 55:11)

MATTHEW 14:30

But when Peter noticed the strong wind, he became frightened, and beginning to sink, he cried out, "Lord, save me!"

One principle of scripture scholarship holds that when a person in a story speaks, the shorter and simpler the statement, the less likely it is to have been embellished by the author. Peter is in a dire situation, and like those times when most of us are in such situations, we express our desires to God in very short phrases. A short phrase like this is called a kerygma, *literally a "kernel" of scripture. It is something that is truly at the heart of the story. As individuals and a church, we reflect upon and enlarge our understanding of God's word, but we must always keep these "kernels" at the heart of it, never losing these clear, concise expressions of our faith.*

PRAYER

Save me, Lord!
When I am afraid,
when I am joyful,
I call to you in faith,
knowing that you hear me
and help me.

LIVING THE PRAYER

Today I will recall or search for a few "kernels" of faith in the scriptures.
Do I have some short phrases of faith handy for the different situations of daily life? What are some that I might use to enrich my prayer?

THE GOSPEL VISION OF THE PROPHETS

Heal me, O LORD, and I shall be healed;
  save me, and I shall be saved;
  for you are my praise.
(Jeremiah 17:14)

Then the disciples approached and said to Jesus, "Do you know that the Pharisees took offense when they heard what you said?"

Jesus is a great role model for many things; standing up to peer pressure could be placed near the top of that list. It's not so much that Jesus didn't care what people thought about him, but he cared more about what God thought about his proclamation of the kingdom. Like his ancestors the prophets, there were times when Jesus did offend those in positions of religious authority. But he didn't make the mistake of thinking that merely being offensive was a sign of being truly prophetic. Above all, Jesus didn't do calculations as to what he might say or do that would win him favor, nor did he calculate what would automatically cause indignation—an example we all would do well to imitate.

PRAYER

Keep me honest, Lord,
for the sake of
sharing the Good News.
Give me a discerning heart;
let me always be open
to the wisdom of your Spirit.

LIVING THE PRAYER

Today I will give witness to God's reign, without calculating what the reaction may be.
Do I choose my words wisely when speaking about my faith? Is it so I can be an authentic witness?

THE GOSPEL VISION OF THE PROPHETS

The prophets prophesy falsely,
    and the priests rule as the prophets direct;
my people love to have it so,
    but what will you do when the end comes?
(Jeremiah 5:31)

MATTHEW 16:19

"I will give you the keys of the kingdom of heaven, and whatever you bind on earth will be bound in heaven, and whatever you loose on earth will be loosed in heaven."

Too often we act like irresponsible adolescents getting the keys to the car. We read the second part of this verse thinking it means we get to make up the rules of heaven. But we don't, any more than a driver's license means we get to make up the rules of the road. To follow Jesus, to accept the authority that was given to him by God, we should read this verse remembering the tremendous responsibility that comes with any kind of authority, and recall (from the Lord's Prayer) that we will also be forgiven by heaven as we have forgiven on earth. It's exciting to get these keys, but we have to drive carefully.

PRAYER
What great trust
you place in me
and all the Church,
God of all power!
Help us all
to follow Jesus' example.

LIVING THE PRAYER

Today I will exercise the authority handed on to me by Jesus in a mature, careful way.
Do I think, self-righteously, that I can control heaven's ways?
How does this get me in trouble spiritually?

THE GOSPEL VISION OF THE PROPHETS

For a child has been born for us,
    a son given to us;
authority rests upon his shoulders;
    and he is named
Wonderful Counselor, Mighty God,
    Everlasting Father, Prince of Peace.
(Isaiah 9:6)

MATTHEW 17:7

But Jesus came and touched them, saying, "Get up and do not be afraid."

On the mountain of the Transfiguration, Jesus is filled with heaven's dazzling light. He stands with the two greatest figures of Israel—Moses and Elijah—who encountered God on Mount Sinai, and God's voice thunders over the whole event. No wonder Peter, James, and John are afraid. These same three would later go into a garden with Jesus. There, from their slumber— as here from their fear—he will tell them again to rise. In both situations, Jesus had a lot going on, but was still able to show compassion for his followers, to strengthen them with the command to rise up, for his is the voice of resurrection. Let us all listen.

PRAYER

Sometimes you overwhelm me
with your majesty,
with what you ask of me.
When I feel that I will fall
under these burdens,
raise me up, O God,
my life and my love.

LIVING THE PRAYER

Today I will allow the hand of Jesus to touch me and raise me up. What experiences have felt overpowering? In what ways could the power of the Resurrection have helped me?

THE GOSPEL VISION OF THE PROPHETS

Do not fear, for I am with you,
    do not be afraid, for I am your God;
I will strengthen you, I will help you,
    I will uphold you with my victorious right hand.
(Isaiah 41:10)

"Take care that you do not despise one of these little ones; for, I tell you, in heaven their angels continually see the face of my Father in heaven."

This verse is a foundation for the belief in guardian angels. Lost along the way has been the scriptural understanding of angels as a conduit for two-way communication between mortals and heaven. They were seen as advocates or petitioners who have "face time" at the throne of grace. If you drew a circle with the word "God" in it and another labeled "mortals" near it, you could draw a third circle that overlapped both and name it "angels." We've lost that sense of the two-way communication through angels, and now tend to limit them to one-way, downward communication only. But Jesus tells us of a loving God who wants to hear from us in every way possible, including through our angels.

PRAYER

I know you send your angels to me,
loving Father.
May I send my angels
to you as well, to tell you
of my great love.

LIVING THE PRAYER

Today I will strengthen my communication with heaven.
How would I draw a chart of the way that heaven and I
communicate? Are angels involved?

THE GOSPEL VISION OF THE PROPHETS

Then the angel of the LORD said, "O LORD of hosts, how long will you withhold mercy from Jerusalem and the cities of Judah, with which you have been angry these seventy years?"
(Zechariah 1:12)

MATTHEW 19:2

Large crowds followed Jesus, and he cured them there.

This bit of information precedes some of the toughest teachings on faithful discipleship that Jesus presents in Matthew: about marriage and divorce, about chastity, about humility, and the need to sell all one's possessions. In a pragmatic way, perhaps Jesus knew that if he worked some signs, like the curing of illness and affliction, it would keep the crowds around. A vice-versa approach may not have been so successful. But what Jesus offers in the teachings that follow these cures is another kind of healing. At first their harshness may seem like God is ripping apart our lives. If so, it is only because the way we have lived is a kind of illness. But through these teachings we can allow a deeper health and wholeness to enter in.

PRAYER

Heal me, help me,
God of mercy,
to find what is weak,
what is wrong in my life
so that your healing grace can
restore me, renew me.

LIVING THE PRAYER

Today I will allow God to "injure" my life, so that I may truly know healing.
From what sort of interior illness or affliction do I suffer? What do I need to do in order for God's healing teaching to enter my life?

THE GOSPEL VISION OF THE PROPHETS

Come, let us return to the LORD;
    for it is he who has torn, and he will heal us;
    he has struck down, and he will bind us up.
(Hosea 6:1)

"Now when the first came, they thought they would receive more; but each of them also received the usual daily wage."

The laborers in the vineyard who toiled the whole day and received the same wage they'd just seen the owner give to those who had worked a few hours would have gotten a sympathetic ear from the older brother in Luke's parable of the prodigal son. Both parables, on the surface, seem to tell us of an unfair (if generous) God who is also, perhaps, unjust. The truest biblical sense of justice is getting what you have coming to you, and not comparing others' treatment with your own. This understanding of justice is behind scripture's portrayal of God as the advocate of all those who do not have equitable treatment from society. Most of us have received what is just; God cares for those who have not.

PRAYER

I spend so much time
focused on how much better
you treat others, my God;
let me turn my gaze inward,
to the generous justice
you show to me.

LIVING THE PRAYER

Today I will act with God's generous, just ways on behalf of those treated unfairly by the world.
How much time do I spend noticing how well God seems to treat others? Do I also evaluate their worthiness compared to my own?

THE GOSPEL VISION OF THE PROPHETS

Learn to do good;
seek justice,
   rescue the oppressed,
defend the orphan,
   plead for the widow.
(Isaiah 1:17)

MATTHEW 21:9

The crowds that went ahead of him and that followed were shouting,

"Hosanna to the Son of David!
Blessed is the one who comes in the name of the Lord!
Hosanna in the highest heaven!"

Every now and then it pays to step back and remember what our acclamations mean. "Hosanna" translates roughly as "Help [or save], I pray." This dramatic scene would have a different impact if we proclaimed "Help us!" instead of "Hosanna!" in our worship. Most of us think of the word "Hosanna" as a generic acclamation of praise. Maybe the Jerusalem crowds did, too. For Christians it is most appropriate that Jesus—whose death and resurrection means salvation—begins the culminating days of his life with crowds of people imploring him in praise to help and save them. When we use "Gloria," "Hallelujah," "Hosanna," or "Amen" to praise and bless Jesus, we also bless the living God who helps us and saves us.

PRAYER

Fill my lips,
fill my heart
with a true and deep
worship of you,
my living God.

LIVING THE PRAYER

Today I will use an acclamation from Sunday worship as my prayer. Do I know the meaning of the words I use in worship? Why is it worth my time to learn about them?

THE GOSPEL VISION OF THE PROPHETS

For all the peoples walk,
each in the name of its god,
but we will walk in the name of the Lord our God
forever and ever.
(Micah 4:5)

MATTHEW 22:39

"And a second commandment is like it: 'You shall love your neighbor as yourself.' "

In commandment language, "love" is an indicator of entry into a covenant. When we hear the two great commandments, this may not be an aspect of "love" that we think about. It isn't the superficial subject of a greeting card; it is a deep, serious, long-term commitment. The covenant love that we must show our neighbor, then, is also much broader and deeper than merely agreeing to be nice to others. Our heartfelt covenant love for others must be a reflection of the covenant love of eternal faithfulness that God offers us.

PRAYER

With all my heart,
soul, and mind
I strive to love you
as you love me, my God.
Help me to love others
as you love them.

LIVING THE PRAYER

Today I will act out of covenant love toward my neighbor.
Who does Jesus say my neighbors are? Can I truly love them as God does?

THE GOSPEL VISION OF THE PROPHETS

But this is the covenant that I will make with the house of Israel after those days, says the LORD: I will put my law within them, and I will write it on their hearts; and I will be their God, and they shall be my people.
(Jeremiah 31:33)

MATTHEW 23:30

"And you say, 'If we had lived in the days of our ancestors, we would not have taken part with them in shedding the blood of the prophets.' "

This chapter contains some Jesus' harshest criticisms of the religious authorities of his day: they do not think they are capable of making their ancestors' mistakes. Whether you say that hindsight is 20-20, or that not knowing your history dooms you to repeat it, this phenomenon of repetition tends to be characteristic of religious individuals and religious institutions. For those who follow Jesus—the one who pointed out this error so clearly—it is doubly grievous when we acknowledge the errors of our ancestors in faith, but rebel against examining our own lives for the same kinds of mistakes. Even when we ask forgiveness for their sins, we can fail to heed Jesus' call to scrutinize our own lives for the same failings.

PRAYER

I honor those
from whom I inherited
the gift of faith, my Lord.
I acknowledge their humanity
and, with your grace,
strive to live the gospel
more fully.

LIVING THE PRAYER

Today I will carefully examine my life for the errors like the ones made by my ancestors in faith.
What situations today mirror previous ones? How can I live the gospel differently today?

THE GOSPEL VISION OF THE PROPHETS

Whether they hear or refuse to hear (for they are a rebellious house), they shall know that there has been a prophet among them. (Ezekiel 2:5)

"But understand this: if the owner of the house had known in what part of the night the thief was coming, he would have stayed awake and would not have let his house be broken into."

In this "mini-parable" Jesus uses some odd analogies: we are innocent homeowners about to be victimized; God is a thief operating stealthily under the cover of night. This fits in with Jesus' overall presentation of the end of time. Everything about it will be unpredictable and unexpected. Of course, once the thief has broken in, there will be mayhem. Perhaps that thief will be breaking into a home filled with darkness that is of our own making. Once inside, perhaps this divine thief will ransack the place for all those possessions we treasured and tried to cling to: our pride, greed, impatience, self-righteousness . . . who knows? Better to be prepared, says Jesus, to live every day already in the light that will come.

PRAYER

Keep me watchful,
ready for the day
that you will come again in glory,
Lord of light!
Shine in my life
today and every day.

LIVING THE PRAYER

Today I will ready my spiritual house by removing one area of darkness.

How prepared would I be if the day of the Lord happened right now? Is my house dark or bright?

THE GOSPEL VISION OF THE PROPHETS

Is not the day of the LORD darkness, not light,
    and gloom with no brightness in it?
(Amos 5:20)

"Then the king will answer them, 'Truly I tell you, just as you did not do it to one of the least of these, you did not do it to me.' "

Gandhi once rather famously observed that he liked Christ, but didn't much like Christians—who were so unlike their Christ. The first people who heard this parable from Jesus would have been stunned to learn of a king who identified so intimately with the lowliest subjects. Gandhi was surprised to encounter a king's subjects who were so hard to identify with the one they claimed as their king. Perhaps it would be a good exercise for us today to try to surprise ourselves into seeing Christ present in those whom we consider outsiders, unworthy, or too lowly to be thought of as our king. If that startles us into action, others will be able to see—not surprisingly—Christ in us.

PRAYER

Help me see you in
the lowly of the world,
so the world may
see you in me,
God, my king.

LIVING THE PRAYER

Today I will surprise myself, seeing Christ present where I had not before.
If I page through the newspaper, or view online news, whom do I see as Christ in the world today? How do I act as a result?

THE GOSPEL VISION OF THE PROPHETS

Do not oppress the widow, the orphan, the alien, or the poor; and do not devise evil in your hearts against one another.
(Zechariah 7:10)

MATTHEW 26:61

"This fellow said, 'I am able to destroy the temple of God and to build it in three days.' "

Do a search on a Bible website for the terms "third day" or "three days" and you will get quite a few results. You'll discover that a number of significant biblical events—Abraham's journey to sacrifice Isaac, Moses on Mount Sinai, as well as the death and resurrection of Jesus—are narrated around or happen on a "third day." All of these contain a major divine intervention, and most of them feature some sort of rescue or saving, as in this verse, where God will "save" the temple, though it has been destroyed. Most of our lives have also had "third day" episodes—whether or not a literal seventy-two hours are involved—in which we knew the saving hand of God.

PRAYER

I trust in your power and presence,
Almighty God;
revive me,
rescue me,
rebuild me
as the temple of your Spirit.
You alone are my Savior.

LIVING THE PRAYER

Today I will recall a "third day" from my life or the life of someone I love.
What are some ways that God has interceded in my life to rescue me? Have I sometimes had to wait longer than three days?

THE GOSPEL VISION OF THE PROPHETS

After two days he will revive us;
on the third day he will raise us up,
that we may live before him.
(Hosea 6:2)

So Joseph took the body of Jesus and wrapped in a clean linen cloth and laid it in his own new tomb, which he had hewn in the rock. He then rolled a great stone to the door of the tomb and went away.

Only Matthew records that Joseph gave Jesus his own tomb; he also makes note (as does John) that it was a new tomb, in which no one else had been laid. The early fathers of the Church pointed out similarities between Jesus' death narratives and birth narratives: a man named Joseph called on to do something unexpected and self-sacrificing; Jesus' body swaddled in linen; his mortal flesh lying in a place (the tomb) where a human body had never been before (Mary's womb). These parallels may have been what Matthew intended, though how much we cannot say. What is clear is that to follow Jesus in life and in death calls upon disciples to give their lives fully, so that God's life may be known.

PRAYER

You bring all life
into the world,
God of the living;
I know you bring life
where our limited sight
can see only death.
All honor and glory to you!

LIVING THE PRAYER

Today I will live my discipleship by offering a self-sacrifice.
Would I make a self-sacrifice for Jesus, as Joseph did? What might that sacrifice be for me?

THE GOSPEL VISION OF THE PROPHETS

For I have no pleasure in the death of anyone, says the Lord God. Turn, then, and live.
(Ezekiel 18:32)

MATTHEW 28:17

When they saw Jesus, they worshiped him; but some doubted.

What, exactly, were they doubting? That Jesus had truly risen? Had truly died? That this actually was him? We'll never know, but we do know that they still worshiped. Given how brief Matthew's post-Resurrection account is, it seems a little unusual to preserve this detail that, even in the presence of the Risen Lord, some of his followers doubted. No matter. The glorified Lord still assures them of his full authority, and commands them to go to every place baptizing and spreading the good news of salvation. Throughout Christian history, worship and doubt have mingled in the hearts of believers. Yet until the day that our worship is perfect in eternity, Jesus sends us out, and is always with us.

PRAYER

Sometimes I am filled
with faith, sometimes with doubt,
but still I worship you,
God of heaven and earth.
Look into the heart you have given me;
see your child there, one who loves you.

LIVING THE PRAYER

Today I will openly admit one doubt I have, and bring it to prayer. What are some things that trouble my life of faith? How would embracing and not avoiding them make my worship more honest, perhaps more fruitful?

THE GOSPEL VISION OF THE PROPHETS

From new moon to new moon,
    and from sabbath to sabbath,
all flesh shall come to worship before me,
says the LORD.
(Isaiah 66:23)

FOLLOWING JESUS WITH MARK
JESUS, HEAVEN'S HUMAN FACE

We know that all four Gospels present Jesus as truly human, but there are some small yet significant ways in which Mark's portrait of him can be said to be the most "human" of them. There is a bluntness in Jesus' speech in Mark that occasionally gets softened by the other evangelists. Jesus is more often impatient or frustrated with the slowness of the disciples to understand what he's trying to do and say. While it is tempting to think that this is a shortcoming in Mark's portrayal of Jesus, it can also be viewed as a strength, a way of honoring his full and true humanity along with his divinity. We can take comfort that his humanity is also a source of his great loving kindness.

PRAYER

Jesus, my friend and brother,
you know my human heart;
I know that you love me.
Be patient with me;
guide me to life with you
in heaven forever.

LIVING THE PRAYER

Today I will honor the fullness of my own humanity as a follower of Jesus.
Do I sometimes think that Jesus doesn't understand my human weaknesses? Am I tempted to focus only on Jesus' divinity? How does this shortchange my life of faith?

THE GOSPEL VISION OF THE PROPHETS

I led them with cords of human kindness,
     with bands of love.
I was to them like those
     who lift infants to their cheeks.
(Hosea 11:4)

MARK 1:7

John the baptizer proclaimed, "The one who is more powerful than I is coming after me; I am not worthy to stoop down and untie the thong of his sandals."

Mark wastes no time in chapter one: we encounter John the Baptist, Jesus is baptized and tempted, calls disciples, teaches in synagogues, and works miraculous healings. Beginning with John the Baptist, everyone in this chapter knows their appropriate relationship to Jesus: disciples follow, unclean spirits convulse, a leper pleads for healing. Important for us, then, is the awareness of our multi-faceted relationship with Jesus. He is more powerful than we, yet we have been filled with his power by baptism; we are followers of his, but also walk by his side. Awareness of the many aspects of our deep, loving relationship to Jesus will enrich our discipleship.

PRAYER

Empower me, my Lord,
to know you and love you
more deeply, more fully;
I call on your name,
I follow you
so that I may lead others to you.

LIVING THE PRAYER

Today I will focus on one relationship with Jesus I have neglected. Do I concentrate only on one or a few of the aspects of my discipleship? How is exploring some others a sign of truly loving Jesus?

THE GOSPEL VISION OF THE PROPHETS

"Therefore I am surely going to teach them, this time I am going to teach them my power and my might, and they shall know that my name is the LORD."
(Jeremiah 16:21)

"No one sews a piece of unshrunk cloth on an old cloak; otherwise, the patch pulls away from it, the new from the old, and a worse tear is made."

Real patches on clothing—the kind meant to cover a rip or a hole—are a rarity nowadays. But this image from Jesus shows us the recurring theme of "old and new" in his teaching. In Jesus' day most everything had to be patched or somehow re-utilized over and over. So this relationship between new and old was important, because it called upon people to be careful stewards. Done improperly, the intended repair ended up actually being bad stewardship. So too with our life of faith. We need to be careful stewards of it, and always attentive to when it needs mending, needs to be renewed in God.

PRAYER

Renew me, Lord,
through your love again;
repair what is broken in me
so that I may live, strong and whole;
restore me to faithfulness
for your glory and your gospel.

LIVING THE PRAYER

Today I will locate a damaged part of my faith life, and repair it. Is there some part of my spirituality that I've asked God to "patch" before? Why is it torn again?

THE GOSPEL VISION OF THE PROPHETS

The Holy Spirit is given as a pledge of our inheritance,
and helps us see our redemption—God's own possession—
to the praise of his glory.
(Ephesians 1:14)

MARK 3:34

And looking at those who sat around him, Jesus said, "Here are my mother and my brothers!"

Overhearing a woman making reference to "my aquarobics family" at the health club prompted reflection on how many groups we refer to as "family" nowadays: our gene pool, circles of close friends, Internet e-cquaintances, faith communities, and so on. This social trend calls into question the genuine closeness or intimacy we can truly communicate with that term, but it is at the heart of Jesus' teaching here. The group surrounding him in this passage could be described as motley: his household, the apostles, those wanting to be dazzled by another miracle . . . and those genuinely wanting to hear of God's reign. When we give ourselves fully to living God's reign, it is the grace of God's reign that truly unites us in the bond we can call family.

PRAYER

When I welcome your reign,
you bless me with others
to share your love;
when I proclaim your reign, Lord,
you strengthen all the bonds
in my life. I give you thanks.

LIVING THE PRAYER

Today I will embrace a new brother or sister in Christ.
Is there someone in my life I have rebuffed whom I should have welcomed? Like Jesus, am I willing to expand the reach of my embrace?

THE GOSPEL VISION OF THE PROPHETS

And what does the LORD require of you
but to do justice, and to love kindness,
and to walk humbly with your God?
(Micah 6:8)

MARK 4:11

And he said to the twelve, "To you has been given the secret of the kingdom of God, but for those outside, everything comes in parables."

There is some tension in certain passages of Mark's Gospel, where the Twelve or the disciples are "insiders" and others need to be invited or brought in. The tension arises when—as with the larger scene this passage comes from—the insiders also need Jesus to explain his parables. We too can think of ourselves as "insiders" who know the "secret" of the kingdom of God; but if we are insiders, then it is our responsibility to be the ones to help outsiders share in this marvelous secret. Perhaps even more effective than the Gospel parables or sacred stories we might share is the parable of God's kingdom that we show in the way we live. Few stories are more easily understood.

PRAYER

How wonderful, O mighty God,
the Good News I have received
in your Son, Jesus Christ!
Let my words and daily living
tell the story of your great love
today and always.

LIVING THE PRAYER

Today I will happily share some "insider" information I have about Jesus.
Can others tell that I have something wonderful to share with them? Do I believe that the Gospel is truly Good News? How can my life be a parable?

THE GOSPEL VISION OF THE PROPHETS

Surely the Lord GOD does nothing
    without revealing his secret
    to his servants the prophets.
(Amos 3:7)

MARK 6:2

On the sabbath he began to teach in the synagogue, and many who heard him were astounded. They said, "Where did this man get all this? What is this wisdom that has been given to him? What deeds of power are being done by his hands!"

It is difficult to put ourselves in the place of those encountering Jesus in the initial days of his public ministry. They thought they knew him, where he came from, who his family was, what he was capable of. Nothing seems to have prepared them for who he really turned out to be. Today we are familiar with Jesus' whole story, yet we can get caught in that same trap, thinking we know him completely, and that he has no surprises left for us. If we're not regularly astounded, we're probably not pursuing our discipleship thoroughly.

PRAYER

Sometimes I mistake
my partial wisdom,
my limited capabilities
for yours, ever-living God.
As I follow Jesus,
may I be willing to grow
beyond my presuppositions.
Let me be astounded by you.

LIVING THE PRAYER

Today I will move past a false assumption that I've made about Jesus or a limitation that I've placed on him.
Do I find life easier if Jesus no longer challenges or astonishes me? How does that limit me as a disciple?

THE GOSPEL VISION OF THE PROPHETS

I will again do
    amazing things with this people,
    shocking and amazing.
The wisdom of their wise shall perish,
    and the discernment of the discerning shall be hidden.
(Isaiah 29:14)

But she answered him, "Sir, even the dogs under the table eat the children's crumbs."

Scripture has a certain admiration for smart-alecks who are willing to question or argue with mighty—even divine—authorities. This tradition goes back to Abraham's challenge of God in Genesis. The psalms that begin with questions (How long, O Lord?) come from this tradition as well. Here Jesus rewards the audacity of the Syro-Phoenecian woman—whose daughter needed healing—by casting out a demon. Another common thread is that these scriptural smart-alecks are often in a position of having little to lose, but much to gain if they are successful. Both the tenacity and the audacity of this woman's faith are things we might do well to emulate in our own relationship with Jesus and the requests we make of him.

PRAYER

Hear me, heal me,
God of power and might!
Help me speak
boldly and bravely in faith,
knowing that in your love for me,
I have an eternity to gain.

LIVING THE PRAYER

Today I will take my prayer "up a notch" in conversation with God. Does my prayer ever have the characteristics of a dialogue or conversation? Do I feel confident enough in my faith to question or challenge? How might I grow in faith this way?

THE GOSPEL VISION OF THE PROPHETS

O LORD, how long shall I cry for help,
    and you will not listen?
Or cry to you "Violence!"
    and you will not save?
(Habakkuk 1:2)

But turning and looking at his disciples, Jesus rebuked Peter and said, "Get behind me, Satan! For you are setting your mind not on divine things but on human things."

Jesus was clearly getting the meaning of his messianic role wrong: having to endure great suffering and rejection. So Peter had the good manners to take him aside and rebuke him privately. Surely Peter felt he could do this, since he had just professed his belief in Jesus as Messiah. But Jesus turns the whole thing public, rebuking Peter for his rebuke, and re-naming Peter, who had just named Jesus "Messiah," as "Satan." This was Peter's second name change during Jesus' public ministry (the first being from Simon to "Peter," the rock). When Peter's actions contradict Jesus' call to follow the divine will, Jesus is ready to leave him behind. Jesus also calls us by name—which one will he use? The answer seems to be up to us.

PRAYER

You named me in the
waters of baptism, mighty God;
I proclaim your greatness.
Let my life show your greatness
in joy, in suffering, until death.

LIVING THE PRAYER

Today I will find Jesus, the Messiah, in some place of suffering or rejection.
Do I only follow Jesus when it's easy? Where can I see his face in those who are marginalized or enduring hardships?

THE GOSPEL VISION OF THE PROPHETS

Trust in the LORD forever,
for in the LORD GOD
you have an everlasting rock.
(Isaiah 26:4)

MARK 9:41

"For truly I tell you, whoever gives you a cup of water to drink because you bear the name of Christ will by no means lose the reward."

Names are certainly important in this part of Mark's Gospel. We've just been through Peter and Jesus' "name-calling," after which we hear about welcoming children in Jesus' name, casting out demons in Jesus' name, and this unusual turn—being cared for because we are named for Christ. Our modern sensibilities forget that a cup of clean, drinkable water in Jesus' world was a very big deal. Mark also wants us to see ourselves in this passage. We have two choices: being the one giving the cup of water, or being the one to whom it is given. Two questions also arise: are others able to see we have been Christ-ened? Do we have the grace and humility to accept the gift they give?

PRAYER

I know your presence in me,
Lord of my life;
increase my humility
and let me find your presence
in those who care for me.

LIVING THE PRAYER

Today I will show forth Christ's presence by allowing another to minister to me.
Am I always focused on doing for others, so they have no opportunity to minister? How do I shortchange their discipleship?

THE GOSPEL VISION OF THE PROPHETS

For I will leave in the midst of you
    a people humble and lowly.
They shall seek refuge in the name of the LORD.
(Zephaniah 3:12)

James and John, the sons of Zebedee, came forward to him and said to him, "Teacher, we want you to do for us whatever we ask of you."

If the Twelve had an inner circle, James and John certainly belonged to it. Even though they had recently experienced Peter (another inner circle member) being scolded by Jesus, they still make this request of him: do our will; reward us with seats in the everlasting inner circle. Their request is self-aggrandizing, but Jesus will ultimately correct this. Their real reward will be to share in his cup of suffering. Those who hold any influence or status—small or great—still risk making this same kind of mistaken request. Even if we think we're not in any sort of "inner circle," we can still lose sight of seeking only God's will when instead we seek our own gratification or glory.

PRAYER

Help me remember,
God of mercy,
that when you allow me to draw
closer to Jesus, it is so that I may
serve others according to your will.
Yours alone is the glory.

LIVING THE PRAYER

Today I will examine my prayer requests carefully for selfishness. Do I ever make selfish requests of Jesus pretending it's for the sake of the gospel? Will Jesus truly answer those prayers?

THE GOSPEL VISION OF THE PROPHETS

See, the Lord God comes with might,
    and his arm rules for him;
his reward is with him,
    and his recompense before him.
(Isaiah 40:10)

"Truly I tell you, if you say to this mountain, 'Be taken up and thrown into the sea,' and if you do not doubt in your heart, but believe that what you say will come to pass, it will be done for you."

Biblical mountains are scenes of epic events, often referred to as godly places. We don't know if Saint Paul, in his discourse on love to the Corinthians, knew this passage from Mark's Gospel when he wrote that faith to move mountains without the ability to live in love is useless. Living in love, like moving mountains, is a tremendously difficult thing to do, if we truly do it in self-giving humility. Here in Mark's Gospel, Jesus is in Jerusalem for his final days, speaking his last words to his followers before, in total faith-filled and self-giving humility, he will not move a mountain, but will walk up one, to show us the ultimate sign of life-giving love.

PRAYER

Let me walk with you,
self-giving God,
in humility and justice;
bring me to your holy mountain.

LIVING THE PRAYER

Today I will perform a small but difficult act of faith.
Am I on the lookout for ways to make grand gestures of faith? How are little deeds, done in quiet love, as important—maybe more important?

THE GOSPEL VISION OF THE PROPHETS

Look at the proud!
Their spirit is not right in them,
but the righteous live by their faith.
(Habakkuk 2:4)

47

MARK 12:25

"For when they rise from the dead, they neither marry nor are given in marriage, but are like angels in heaven."

Throughout Christian history we have used things of earthly life— beautiful music, grand buildings, foods we enjoy, people we love— to describe eternal life. But limited things cannot truly express resurrected life. They are gifts from heaven; they are not necessarily our reward in heaven. The lyric "In heaven there is no beer/that's why we drink it here" may be closer to the truth! There is also a kind of consumerist selfishness in thinking our personal "heaven" will be customized. To be joined with ALL the angels and saints (even those saints we didn't like much on earth) in the everlasting glory of God is a boundless joy, worthy of our contemplation. It also calls us to live "beyond" ourselves in the here and now.

PRAYER

In this life, Lord,
I merely glimpse
the joy and glory
that await me
in the life I will share
with the company of heaven
and you eternally.

LIVING THE PRAYER

Today I will stop thinking of something I enjoy as a heavenly reward awaiting me.
Is there one "thing" I secretly hope awaits me? How would I describe heaven to someone who is not Christian?

THE GOSPEL VISION OF THE PROPHETS

Thus says the LORD:
Heaven is my throne
    and the earth is my footstool;
what is the house that you would build for me,
    and what is my resting place?
(Isaiah 66:1)

"But about that day or hour no one knows, neither the angels in heaven, nor the Son, but only the Father."

Bible codes have become very popular. Perhaps it is the increasing fascination of the modern mind in the past few centuries with the precision of equations and formulas. Bible codes have built upon a broader movement begun in the nineteenth century to read parts of the Gospels, Revelation, and some Hebrew prophets as keys to current events that would give mere mortals knowledge about the end of time—a time about which Jesus himself said not even the angels or the Son knew. Jesus counsels a different approach: we are to live in a constant state of readiness. This should be a source of comfort, not anxiety. If we continually live according to the gospel, we will be ready to greet Jesus with joy when he comes again.

PRAYER

I watch and wait,
alert for your coming,
and to your presence
in the world around me.
Maran Atha!
Come, Lord!

LIVING THE PRAYER

Today I will live so I can greet the Lord serenely and with elation. What will I be doing today? If the Lord were to return today, would I try to scramble to live differently? Would I be calm?

THE GOSPEL VISION OF THE PROPHETS

On that day the LORD their God will save them
    for they are the flock of his people;
for like the jewels of a crown
    they shall shine on his land.
(Zechariah 9:16)

MARK 14:26

When they had sung the hymn, they went out to the
Mount of Olives.

*If there was a quiz as to what Jesus and his disciples did between
the Last Supper and going to the Mount of Olives (where the
subsequent events of his passion would begin), it is doubtful that
anyone would answer, "They sang a hymn." But this is how the
Passover meal would have concluded. These two great acts of
Jesus' self-gift—giving himself in bread and wine; giving himself
in the sacrifice of the cross—are appropriately connected by
the act of those present offering themselves in praise to God. To
sing their praise of God (Hallel Ya in Hebrew), Jesus and his
followers had to give of their very breath, an act Jesus would
soon repeat, giving his final breath on the cross.*

PRAYER

Help me to live
as your Son Jesus did,
giving of my very self
for the sake of others
and in songs of praise
to you, God of love.

LIVING THE PRAYER

*Today I will give praise aloud to God, focused on the gift of my
breath.*
Am I ready to praise God even when I am surrounded by
events that trouble or threaten me? How could Jesus sing as he
faced his death?

THE GOSPEL VISION OF THE PROPHETS

But I with the voice of thanksgiving
    will sacrifice to you;
what I have vowed I will pay.
    Deliverance belongs to the LORD!
(Jonah 2:9)

MARK 15:34

At three o'clock Jesus cried out with a loud voice, "Eloi, Eloi, lema sabachthani?" which means, "My God, my God, why have you forsaken me?"

Aside from describing this cry of Jesus as "loud" we have no clue as to how Jesus cried out this line from the psalms. Was it in desperation, hoping for a last-minute divine rescue? Angry, that this was the reward for faithfully ministering and proclaiming the kingdom? Challenging, in keeping with the spirit of Israel's many questioning laments? A final voice of praise? Perhaps it was some mixture of all these. We cannot know, for scripture is silent on the matter. It is an expression of the deeply intimate, loving relationship that can voice emotions this deep, and a commitment as deep as the one Jesus lived. In a few verses, Jesus will cry out loudly again, this time wordlessly, as he breathes his last.

PRAYER

Do you ever forsake
or forget me, my God?
Even in those times
when I think this is so,
may I still cry out to you.

LIVING THE PRAYER

Today I will call out to God—on my own behalf or another's—even if God seems absent.
When have I felt abandoned by God? Who else does God seem to have forgotten? How can I have this attitude and still be faithful?

THE GOSPEL VISION OF THE PROPHETS

Why have you forgotten us completely?
Why have you forsaken us these many days?
(Lamentations 5:20)

So they went out and fled from the tomb, for terror and amazement had seized them; and they said nothing to anyone, for they were afraid.

This verse is generally acknowledged to be the original ending of Mark's Gospel, though nobody is certain why the Gospel may have ended here. But imagine that you are an early Christian, those first followers of Jesus still around you, who have shared the stories of Jesus' post-Resurrection appearances and ascension. Someone reading Mark's Gospel from a scroll rolls it up and stops here. A slight smile lights your face, for you know that's not *the end of the story! This is the life of the disciple, no matter what we encounter as we strive to live the gospel. Success or failure, we are heirs of that smile, for we know the true end of the story: that, ultimately, we have no cause for fear.*

PRAYER

I trust in you,
ever-faithful God;
fill me with courage,
confident in the resurrection
of your Son, who now lives
with you and the Holy Spirit
forever and ever.

LIVING THE PRAYER

Today I will smile in faith, and share the life-giving story of my faith.
Do I sometimes keep silent about my beliefs out of fear? Am I able to look past current circumstances to the real end of the gospel story?

THE GOSPEL VISION OF THE PROPHETS

You came near when I called on you;
     you said, "Do not fear!"
(Lamentations 3:57)

FOLLOWING JESUS WITH LUKE
JESUS, SENT BY THE SPIRIT

Luke is the evangelist who mentions the Holy Spirit and articulates the work of the Holy Spirit most often, both in his Gospel and in Acts of the Apostles. In the story of Jesus' birth, not only is his mother, Mary, filled with the Spirit, but all those who appear in these stories—Elizabeth, Zechariah, Simeon— are under the Spirit's power as well. While Jesus manifests little of the behavior we often associate with the Spirit's presence— ecstatic speech, for instance—the steadfastness of his mission is a certain indicator of the ongoing power of the Spirit. "The Spirit of the Lord is upon me," Jesus announces early in his public ministry. Day by day, may we be able to announce the same Spirit upon us.

PRAYER

In you, Lord Jesus, I see the Spirit
at work in my life:
> the Spirit of life in my birth
> the Spirit of grace in my baptism
> the Spirit of power in my witness
> the Spirit of your glad tidings
> > of salvation.

LIVING THE PRAYER

Today I will know the Spirit's presence in my dedication to the gospel.
Do I think only external displays are signs of the Spirit at work? In what other, less visible ways might the Spirit want others to see Jesus in me?

THE GOSPEL VISION OF THE PROPHETS

I will never again hide my face from them, when I pour out my spirit upon the house of Israel, says the Lord GOD.
(Ezekiel 39:29)

The angel replied, "I am Gabriel. I stand in the presence of God, and I have been sent to speak to you and to bring you this good news."

Gabriel's a busy angel. Though he appears in both testaments of the Bible, he's named more often and is more active in the sacred literature written between the two (but not included in the Bible). Muslims also believe that the Qur'an was revealed to Muhammed through Gabriel, and Baha'i holds him to be the very manifestation of the Divine Spirit on earth. It is appropriate that this hard-working messenger of God—an agent of God's strength (which is what his name means) made known on earth—would be the one to bring Mary her good news. In his own ministry, Jesus was also a very busy messenger of the reign of God being manifested and revealed everywhere.

PRAYER

I stand before you, O God,
ready to serve as your messenger.
Send me, as you sent your Son,
to speak good news of salvation
everywhere, to everyone.

LIVING THE PRAYER

Today I will step up my activity as a messenger of God's good news. Am I a busy or lazy messenger? Do I excuse myself because I am not an archangel?

THE GOSPEL VISION OF THE PROPHETS

How beautiful upon the mountains
    are the feet of the messenger who announces peace,
who brings good news,
    who announces salvation,
    who says to Zion, "Your God reigns."
(Isaiah 52:7)

Jesus said to Mary and Joseph, "Why were you searching for me? Did you not know that I must be in my Father's house?"

For someone who stated at the outset of his Gospel that he wants to write an "orderly account," Luke leaves a stretch of undocumented time between Jesus' being lost and then found after three days in Jerusalem and the beginning of his public ministry. Luke tells us only that Jesus increased in wisdom and years until we meet him again, two chapters later, as an adult. But rather than wasting our own time searching for the lost details of these years, we will find Jesus when we also go to his Father's house, the house of God's reign of truth, mercy, justice, beauty, and grace. It is certain that whenever we look into that house, there we will find Jesus.

PRAYER

Lead me to your house,
my loving Father;
with Jesus may I be found there,
seeking your wisdom,
living in the joy of your reign
all the days of my life.

LIVING THE PRAYER

Today I will search for Jesus' presence in a place I might not normally look.
Aside from the church where I worship, where else might the "house" of Jesus' Father be? Am I truly dedicated to making my search for Jesus far-ranging?

THE GOSPEL VISION OF THE PROPHETS

When you search for me, you will find me; if you seek me with all your heart, I will let you find me, says the LORD.
(Jeremiah 29:13–14)

"Bear fruits worthy of repentance. Do not begin to say to yourselves, 'We have Abraham as our ancestor'; for I tell you, God is able from these stones to raise up children to Abraham."

This teaching from John the Baptist (Jesus doesn't speak at all in this chapter of Luke) shows him as a prophetic herald of the coming ministry of Jesus. John illustrates that discipleship has demands: true repentance is not merely a passive act of express- ing regret, but it is an active turning around of our lives, in order to bear worthy fruit. He also deflates those who self-righteously think their religious pedigree is some sort of guarantee of God's favor. It is the life actively lived in justice that is the sign of God's presence in one's life; God judges us to be upright through our ongoing willingness to turn from sin and re-dedicate our lives to the Good News.

PRAYER

I turn to you, Lord,
I turn away from sin;
help me to bear fruit—
mercy, truth, peace, justice—
so that all may come to know
the wonder of your salvation.

LIVING THE PRAYER

Today I will actively follow up on an act of repentance.
In what way have I repented lately? Has my repentance borne any fruit?

THE GOSPEL VISION OF THE PROPHETS

Zion shall be redeemed by justice,
    and those in her who repent, by righteousness.
(Isaiah 1:27)

Then Jesus stood over her and rebuked the fever, and it left her. Immediately she got up and began to serve them.

There has been a trend in holistic treatment of illness to personify illnesses, especially critical ones. Cancer patients and their families, for example, are encouraged to express their feelings in letters written to the disease. It's the sort of healing activity that Jesus works here, when he doesn't merely cure Peter's mother-in-law, but rebukes her fever, as he rebuked Satan in the desert. We have a better understanding of the physiological origins of disease today, but can't allow that to diminish the personal dimensions of healing. Though her immediate serving at table has generated claims of sexism in recent times, for Luke this is an indicator of the immediacy and potency of Jesus' healing power. The disease, the healing, and her service—it's all personal.

PRAYER
....

How marvelous is your
healing power, mighty God!
May I bravely name
what is unhealthy in me,
so that you may restore me
for the service of your people.

LIVING THE PRAYER

Today I will rebuke a personal ailment in the name of Jesus.
Even if I don't suffer from chronic or serious physical illness, how am I in need of healing? Do I have the faith to call out my ailment by name?

THE GOSPEL VISION OF THE PROPHETS

And the LORD said to Satan, "The LORD rebuke you, O Satan! The LORD who has chosen Jerusalem rebuke you!"
(Zechariah 3:2)

LUKE 5:16

But he would withdraw to deserted places and pray.

It's comforting to know that even the Son of God had to get away by himself every now and then to recharge. When we think that our busy-ness, our stress, is a reason to stop personal prayer, or that our one weekly hour of community prayer will take care of everything spiritual, we need to remember this example from Jesus. The stream of people coming for healing, the needs or demands of his chosen followers and the growing number of followers he attracted, the increasing conflicts with religious authorities as his stature grew—all of these could have given him a stress-filled schedule that would put ours to shame. Yet the Son of God withdrew, by himself, to pray. As true disciples of his, we need to show that prayer is a priority by setting aside time and putting our lives on hold for it.

PRAYER

Lord, I'm busy;
you have given me
so much to do, so many people
that they crowd you out.
Help me re-order my life,
to place you at its heart.

LIVING THE PRAYER

Today I will do a careful accounting of the time I spend.
Is there one activity today I can abandon in order to pray? What things am I counting more important than personal prayer?

THE GOSPEL VISION OF THE PROPHETS

Then Jonah prayed to the LORD his God from the belly of the fish. (Jonah 2:1)

"Woe to you who are full now,
  for you will be hungry.
Woe to you who are laughing now,
  for you will mourn and weep."

Luke's version of the Beatitudes is understandably less popular than Matthew's, which doesn't have that whole "woe" section. It's easier to hear Jesus tell us who is blessed and say "That's me!" (even when it isn't). Jesus' "woe" theme here is consistent with much of his teaching regarding the coming reign of God: we shouldn't mistake our earthly success or happiness for a guarantee of those same things in eternity. When we think our full bellies are our salvation, or that our laughter—sometimes at the expense of others—will last forever, we have another thing coming, Jesus says. True joy and unfailing contentment are signs of those who have deeply and truly embraced the glad tidings of Jesus.

PRAYER

Let my joys and pleasures
come from you alone, my God;
keep me from pride
and self-assuredness,
to live out and welcome in
your holy, everlasting reign.

LIVING THE PRAYER

Today I will not jump to conclusions about others by laughing at them or demeaning those in want.
Do I think I am superior to others, or think God favors me more? In what ways are these judgments of mine manifested, judgments that belong to God alone?

THE GOSPEL VISION OF THE PROPHETS

Woe to them, for they have strayed from me!
  Destruction to them, for they have rebelled against me!
(Hosea 7:13)

LUKE 7:36

One of the Pharisees asked Jesus to eat with him, and he went into the Pharisee's house and took his place at the table.

Be careful what you ask for. In this Pharisee's house, Jesus' feet received anointing by the ointment, tears, tresses, and kisses of a sinful woman (NOT Mary Magdalene, it must be stated). Thinking that a true prophet of God would forbid or be repulsed by this act, the Pharisee (Jesus' dinner host) admonishes him and subsequently gets a resounding reprimand disguised as a teaching. When we invite Jesus into our lives, we can't assume it's always going to be a comfy, cozy encounter. Though we invite him to be our guest, we must always remember that he will be the host at the table where we hope to be seated in heaven.

PRAYER

Let me welcome you
into my life,
you who invite me
time and time again
to your feast of salvation here,
and to your eternal banquet.

LIVING THE PRAYER

Today I will extend an invitation to someone I don't tend to spend time with.
Whom do I avoid, thinking Christ cannot be present in them? What might Christ teach me through them?

THE GOSPEL VISION OF THE PROPHETS

On this mountain the LORD of hosts will make for all peoples
        a feast of rich food, a feast of well-aged wines,
of rich food filled with marrow, of well-aged wines strained clear.
(Isaiah 25:6)

LUKE 8:55

And her spirit returned, and she got up at once. Then Jesus directed them to give her something to eat.

Many scholars have pointed out stories of pagan deities who were revivified or resurrected from the dead. But the stories of those figures tend to be self-contained; they return from the dead for their own sake. In Luke's recounting of Jesus raising the daughter of Jairus from the dead, we see the might of God's life in Jesus' own resurrection already at work. Like Jesus would be on Calvary, this little girl is truly dead. And, as in Jesus' post-Resurrection appearances, it is a meal that helps confirm that she is truly back from the dead. In a similar way, the power of the Resurrection, given to us at baptism, is not given to us only for ourselves, but for others and the world.

PRAYER

Spirit of everlasting life,
in the waters of baptism
you gave me eternal life
in Jesus Christ, a grace to share
so that all will know you to be
the true and living God.

LIVING THE PRAYER

Today I will share the life of Christ, rather than keep it to myself. What people or situations around me are in need of reviving? How can I let the power of the Resurrection be channeled through me?

THE GOSPEL VISION OF THE PROPHETS

But the Lord is the true God;
    he is the living God and the everlasting King.
(Jeremiah 10:10)

LUKE 9:51

When the days drew near for him to be taken up, he set his face to go to Jerusalem.

For any reader who knows the whole story of the gospel—for disciples in particular—this passage from Luke should send chills up the spine. We can imagine Jesus turning toward Jerusalem, place of his destiny, resolutely setting his face to go there. Jerusalem will be the place of his trial and abandonment. Jerusalem, whose own daughters will weep and will be told by Jesus that they will pray to be childless. Jerusalem, where God's will for Jesus must reign supreme, as must Jesus himself. Luke reminds us, at the beginning of this fearsome part of his Gospel, that ultimately it is to be "taken up," to ascend to heaven, that is the truest destiny of Jesus, and for his disciples.

PRAYER

Be with me, Lord,
as I continue my daily journey
to whatever future you call me.
Let me always keep my face
turned toward you.

LIVING THE PRAYER

Today, with Jesus at my side, I will face a situation that I have been avoiding.
What are difficulties that I have avoided or denied in the past? How has this kept me from truly following Jesus?

THE GOSPEL VISION OF THE PROPHETS

Look, O LORD, and consider!
    To whom have you done this?
Should women eat their offspring,
    the children they have borne?
Should priest and prophet be killed
    in the sanctuary of the Lord?
(Lamentations 2:20)

LUKE 10:21

At that same hour Jesus rejoiced in the Holy Spirit and said, "I thank you, Father, Lord of heaven and earth, because you have hidden these things from the wise and the intelligent and have revealed them to infants; yes, Father, for such was your gracious will."

This seems like an odd time for Jesus to be rejoicing in the Holy Spirit. Wouldn't it make more sense for him to be having second thoughts about heading for Jerusalem? Or at least sweating over his decision? Shouldn't the enemies of Jesus, trying to trip him up or catch him in blasphemy, be the ones rejoicing that he's headed for Jerusalem? Jesus' answer to all of this is "no." Though the Gospel honestly presents us with the tough side of discipleship, we are fortified with reminders that God's will comes first, not ours; that many times our expectations will be turned upside down; that Pentecost's outpouring of the Spirit is always upon us. Rejoice!

PRAYER

Your will be done, my Father.
Give me wisdom,
make me joyful
every day of the journey
you have set before me.

LIVING THE PRAYER

Today I will be joyful about a difficult decision, past or present.
Is a grudging, dour acceptance of God's will true acceptance?
Can I rejoice in the challenging things that God demands?

THE GOSPEL VISION OF THE PROPHETS

Do not rejoice over me, O my enemy;
    when I fall, I shall rise;
when I sit in darkness,
    the LORD will be a light to me.
(Micah 7:8)

"And forgive us our sins,

for we ourselves forgive everyone indebted to us.
And do not bring us to the time of trial."

Sins? Debts? Trespasses? Trial or temptation? Few Gospel passages are as familiar as the Lord's Prayer. Most Christians probably know this verse in some form of "Forgive us _____ as we forgive _____." But getting overly focused on which particular terms we're using can make us miss the point: this is a dangerous contract agreement to make with God. Perhaps there was a tinge of irony in Jesus' voice as he gave this prayer instruction, "for we ourselves forgive . . .", knowing full well that we often don't. Perhaps the "trial" here isn't only some sort of temptation or testing, but also that final judgment trial we will undergo, when God decides if we truly have lived up to this contract we have prayed so often.

PRAYER

I tremble, O Lord,
as I ask you to forgive me.
Grant me your own
merciful, all-forgiving heart;
help me to live,
ready to meet you at the end.

LIVING THE PRAYER

Today I will recall a time (or times) when I failed to forgive. Am I able to rectify any of the situations when I failed to forgive? How prepared am I to pray the Lord's Prayer, knowing I've asked God to act as I have acted?

THE GOSPEL VISION OF THE PROPHETS

And so people are humbled,
and everyone is brought low—
do not forgive them!
(Isaiah 2:9)

LUKE 12:56

"You hypocrites! You know how to interpret the appearance of earth and sky, but why do you not know how to interpret the present time?"

It must have been frustrating for Jesus—he, the ultimate sign of the reign of God—to have people continually looking around him or through him. Perhaps more frustrating to have them get caught up in the razzle-dazzle surface of his miracles without looking deeply into what they meant: God wants to heal, forgive, embrace, restore, and revive . . . and so must we. Today we still do a good job of watching weather patterns (on TV or the Internet), and a better job of tracking our finances. But we skim over the headline about the poor, mute the TV report about powerless victims, click away from the hunger statistics over to celebrity news video. We still fail to see Jesus present in our time.

PRAYER

The signs are all around me,
but I often ignore them.
Perhaps they are signals
of your kingdom, Lord,
that I don't want to see.
Make me aware and alert.

LIVING THE PRAYER

Today I will focus on a particular place the reign of God is at work in my world.
What kinds of news stories or websites get my time and attention? Which people or events dominate my conversation?

THE GOSPEL VISION OF THE PROPHETS

This is the sign to you from the LORD, that the LORD will do this thing that he has promised.
(Isaiah 38:7)

LUKE 13:30

"Indeed, some are last who will be first, and some are first who will be last."

This would be a lot more airtight if Jesus hadn't put that "some" in the middle of it all. Those who are looking for a quick and easy, absolute guarantee from him are going to be disappointed. Jesus knew that to make oneself "last" for the purpose of being first at some later time would be to do it for the wrong reason. He is speaking, of course, about our humility, our readiness to seek and do God's will, our willingness to live for others. People who are low or high in earthly station are capable of living as true disciples. It is a mistake to think that the status or surface of any person's life is a foolproof indicator of one's heavenly destiny.

PRAYER

You bless me and favor me greatly,
your hand always open;
let this be a source of my humility
and my desire to put others first
as you do, my loving Lord.

LIVING THE PRAYER

Today I will live as one who is last or least, putting others first. In terms of the whole world, am I a "last" or a "first" person? Am I more concerned with my status compared to others than with how I live?

THE GOSPEL VISION OF THE PROPHETS

For from the least to the greatest of them,
    everyone is greedy for unjust gain;
and from prophet to priest,
    everyone deals falsely.
(Jeremiah 6:13)

LUKE 14:27

"Whoever does not carry the cross and follow me cannot be my disciple."

As Jesus continues his journey to Jerusalem, he seems compelled to make it very clear that this is not a journey for wimps. What following Jesus as a disciple will entail is not always that clear, especially when it comes to the crosses that life might present. It's even more difficult when we know that choosing to follow Jesus faithfully will place a cross upon us. Here Jesus speaks this admonition in the midst of some other harsh directives: we cannot be disciples if we do not hate our immediate family members, we cannot be disciples if we are not ready to give up all our possessions. To follow Jesus is to accept the cross that he is headed for, our eyes forward, only on him.

PRAYER
....

You have given me crosses,
and there are more to come;
I know this, O Lord.
Let me bear them with your strength
as I continue to follow you faithfully.

LIVING THE PRAYER

Today I will embrace, rather than try to avoid, a cross in my life. Have there been times my discipleship has not been faithful, because I knew it would entail a cross? Is there a way to get back on track?

THE GOSPEL VISION OF THE PROPHETS

Yet they did not obey or incline their ear, but, in the stubbornness of their evil will, they walked in their own counsels, and looked backward rather than forward.
(Jeremiah 7:24)

LUKE 15:20

"But while he was still far off, his father saw him and was filled with compassion; he ran and put his arms around him and kissed him."

We might wonder which of the prodigal father's two sons was more surprised: the runaway son who figured he'd be lucky not to be slain or enslaved upon his return, or the faithful one who figured his brother would be slain or enslaved. One is startled by compassion, an embrace, a kiss—the other by music, dancing, a feast. No matter which son we identify with, the lesson is that when we—or others—return to the Father, it is not a time of death or enslavement. Our time of return to the Father is also the time of his return to our lives. Whatever events led to separation, they are obliterated by the joy and celebration caused by the return.

PRAYER

What joy you must feel
when I return to you,
my loving Father!
You run to meet me,
hold me, kiss me in welcome.
Let me share fully
in your joy.

LIVING THE PRAYER

Today I will be joyful about someone's return to God's embrace.
Do I celebrate when others have overcome a spiritual obstacle?
Why or why not?

THE GOSPEL VISION OF THE PROPHETS

Therefore say to them, Thus says the LORD of hosts: Return to me, says the LORD of hosts, and I will return to you, says the LORD of hosts.
(Zechariah 1:3)

LUKE 16:31

"Abraham said to the rich man, 'If they do not listen to Moses and the prophets, neither will they be convinced even if someone rises from the dead.' "

This disturbing conclusion to the story of the poor beggar named Lazarus at the gate of the rich man helps place this colorful story into its larger framework about the relationship between earthly life and life everlasting. It may seem that "help the poor or else" is the point. By bringing in Abraham, Moses, and the prophets, Jesus weaves together Israel's moral/ethical code with belief in the resurrection. Some believed that, since wealth was a sign of God's favor, only the wealthy would be resurrected. But Jesus teaches that to rest in the bosom of Abraham in eternity, we must first shine with that resurrected eternal life here and now.

PRAYER

Let your everlasting light
shine in me,
shine through me, my God,
until that day
you bring me to eternal rest.

LIVING THE PRAYER

Today I will be a living reflection of the justice of eternal life.
Do I act justly only out of fear? How can I act justly for better reasons?

THE GOSPEL VISION OF THE PROPHETS

For I know how many are your transgressions,
    and how great are your sins—
you who afflict the righteous, who take a bribe,
    and push aside the needy in the gate.
(Amos 5:12)

LUKE 17:3

"Be on your guard! If another disciple sins, you must rebuke the offender, and if there is repentance, you must forgive."

On guard against what? In speaking of the sin-rebuke-repentance-forgiveness chain of events Jesus was exercising keen insight into human nature, a nature he fully possessed: we can short-circuit this process before it has been completed. To allow sin without rebuke, to rebuke without openness to repentance, to experience repentance but not forgive, all are ways to halt the path to reconciliation. We must also be on guard to make this a community process, noting that Jesus keeps the entire process between disciples. It is in the community of believers that sin occurs, and also in that community that the restoration through reconciliation must happen. It's not easy for human nature to work in divine ways. Be on guard!

PRAYER

How boundless your mercy,
God of forgiveness.
Keep me open to the
work of compassion
in my life and the lives
of those around me.

LIVING THE PRAYER

Today I will finish the reconciliation process where I have left it incomplete.
Do I avoid those I must face for true reconciliation? How does this thwart God's mercy?

THE GOSPEL VISION OF THE PROPHETS

I will cleanse them from all the guilt of their sin against me, and I will forgive all the guilt of their sin and rebellion against me. (Jeremiah 33:8)

"Indeed, it is easier for a camel to go through the eye of a needle than for someone who is rich to enter the kingdom of God."

Real camel. Real needle. Many attempts have been made to spiritualize or explain away this difficult saying. Some have said it's about a gate in the Jerusalem wall, or rock formations that are small and narrow (but still camel-passable). More rare, but an even bigger reach, is the position that the Aramaic word turned into the Greek for "camel" really meant a household domesticated animal (which still wouldn't go through a needle's eye very easily). When we try to diminish this saying of Jesus, we are making ourselves in the image of the rich ruler, saddened to find out he must abandon his wealth to enter the kingdom. It truly takes all our effort to follow Jesus, and not be led by earthly possessions.

PRAYER

As I try to follow you,
I stumble over the things
that I want but don't need.
Help me to abandon these,
desiring only to follow you, Lord.

LIVING THE PRAYER

Today I will give up a possession that places unhealthy demands on me.
Will I, one day, be able to pass through that needle's eye? What distracts me as I try to enter heaven's narrow gate?

THE GOSPEL VISION OF THE PROPHETS

Moreover, wealth is treacherous;
    the arrogant do not endure.
They open their throats wide as Sheol;
    like Death they never have enough.
(Habakkuk 2:5)

LUKE 19:3

Zaccheus was trying to see who Jesus was, but on account of the crowd he could not, because he was short in stature.

In a few more verses, Jesus will enter Jerusalem and begin the confrontations that will ultimately lead to his suffering and death. So the Zaccheus story seems light-hearted, perhaps frivolous. In the coming scenes, the crowds will be important, so maybe we can learn something from Zaccheus. Though he was socially and economically a big man, he was short. But he was long on initiative, climbing the tree to see Jesus, hosting Jesus as his guest, willing to right any wrong he had committed. Who in those crowds would have done the same? As we follow Jesus to Jerusalem, will we let the crowds who are merely curious or angry get in our way? Will we have the strength and courage to follow him?

PRAYER

Other people get between us,
so sometimes I just give up
and walk away.
Help me to be strong, resourceful,
with the courage to follow,
doing your Father's will, Lord.

LIVING THE PRAYER

Today I will not be swayed by others who distract my discipleship. What do I do because "everyone" does it, though disciples shouldn't? What talents do I possess that give me the ability to overcome this temptation?

THE GOSPEL VISION OF THE PROPHETS

Can your courage endure, or can your hands remain strong in the days when I shall deal with you? I the LORD have spoken, and I will do it.
(Ezekiel 22:14)

LUKE 20:37

"And the fact that the dead are raised Moses himself showed, in the story about the bush, where he speaks of the Lord as the God of Abraham, the God of Isaac, and the God of Jacob."

Some of the beliefs surrounding resurrection that we commonly accept today—heaven/hell, body/soul, eternal life/damnation— were still in a state of flux during Jesus' time. There was not a unified way of thinking about these things. Even the idea of an afterlife spent in some other place or reality was not a uniform belief. It is no surprise that Luke presents major debates about these matters just before Jesus is to face his passion and death. Judaism largely believed there were two choices: life in the covenant or death by breaking the covenant. Though Jesus was to die, he showed that being completely faithful to the covenant— as were Israel's patriarchs Abraham, Isaac, and Jacob— ultimately leads through death to life.

PRAYER

Loving God,
keep me faithful
to the new covenant in Christ.
Help me follow him through death
to life everlasting.

LIVING THE PRAYER

Today I will recall a time that faithfulness eventually led me to life. Can I see past the immediate? Does my belief in God's faithfulness strengthen my own?

THE GOSPEL VISION OF THE PROPHETS

And to this people you shall say: Thus says the LORD: See, I am setting before you the way of life and the way of death. (Jeremiah 21:8)

LUKE 21:8

And Jesus said, "Beware that you are not led astray; for many will come in my name and say, 'I am he!' and, 'The time is near!' Do not go after them."

What Jesus is warning against is idols. In our culture—which often thinks of idols as good things—it is important to remember that, in spiritual terms, an idol is anything or anyone who stands in the way between God and us. The idols that Jesus speaks of are those people who do not consistently point away from themselves and toward the divine, but make themselves the focal point. The same goes for those who claim that they know things only known to God, such as the final time of fulfillment. Our job is to "beware"—to be wary of anyone who claims himself or herself as the object we should focus on, who claims to be able to predict the last day.

PRAYER

Keep my heart,
my eyes, and my mind
centered on you alone,
God of my life.
Make me turn away from
those who lead me astray.

LIVING THE PRAYER

Today I will examine my life for idols and refocus my relationships to them.
Are there people in my spiritual life who might become "idols" for me? How might they lead me away from Christ?

THE GOSPEL VISION OF THE PROPHETS

For those who led this people led them astray,
and those who were led by them were left in confusion.
(Isaiah 9:16)

But Jesus said to him, "Judas, is it with a kiss that you are betraying the Son of Man?"

It is doubtful that this fateful scene recounts the first time that Judas had kissed Jesus. For those closest to Jesus, embracing and kissing would have been commonplace forms of greeting, an expression of familiarity and unity. But Luke tells us earlier in this chapter that Satan had entered into Judas' heart, and so the powers of darkness were now directing this act of closeness. As in much of his public ministry, it is the outward action contradicted by the heart's intent that Jesus points out. It is still possible for followers of Jesus today to have the powers of darkness in us, even when our outward actions appear to be those of faithful disciples. For us, as it was with Judas, this is betrayal.

PRAYER

Let me look
deeply into my own heart
with your eyes, O Lord.
May I discover there
a true love of you
to lead me in living
honestly and faithfully.

LIVING THE PRAYER

Today I will bring my heart and actions into unity for my life of faith.
What gestures of faith do I make that are dishonest or empty?
Which needs to change: my heart or my actions?

THE GOSPEL VISION OF THE PROPHETS

O Jerusalem, wash your heart clean of wickedness
    so that you may be saved.
How long shall your evil schemes
    lodge within you?
(Jeremiah 4:14)

Then Jesus said, "Father, forgive them; for they do not know what they are doing." And they cast lots to divide his clothing.

The omission of the first part of this verse in a number of the oldest manuscripts of Luke has interested everyone from serious scripture scholars to people attempting to give Jesus a makeover as someone vindictive, bent on retribution. These words of Jesus are central to the way Christians remember his death; they were for Stephen, in Acts, when he met his death. They also are central to the way Jesus lived his life, and they reflect the way that God deals with us daily in our own living. Throughout the Gospel, in his actions and the parables he told, Jesus consistently showed a just, merciful God who doesn't deny our wrongdoing but is always prepared to forgive.

PRAYER

I have sinned, my God,
toward you and my neighbor.
I know you are just and merciful;
help me know your forgiveness
so I will sin no more.

LIVING THE PRAYER

Today I will ask for or extend forgiveness in a difficult situation. What situation in my life remains unreconciled? How can the assurance of God's pardon not be turned into an encouragement to sin?

THE GOSPEL VISION OF THE PROPHETS

Who is a God like you, pardoning iniquity
    and passing over the transgression
    of the remnant of your possession?
He does not retain his anger forever,
    because he delights in showing clemency.
(Micah 7:18)

But they urged him strongly, saying, "Stay with us, because it is almost evening and the day is now nearly over." So he went in to stay with them.

There could have been many reasons the two disciples on the road to Emmaus urged the risen Lord (whom they did not yet recognize) to stay with them. It could have been the extraordinary explanation he had given of the events surrounding his own death, or the simple fact that it was dangerous for anyone to travel alone after dark. It does not matter what prompts us to urge Jesus to stay with us, only that we ask. For us as for them, the reward for that invitation is that he will once again be revealed to us, so our hearts will burn within, so we will understand what had once been frightening, so we will not fear the dark of any night.

PRAYER

Stay with me,
remain with me,
reveal yourself to me,
gracious God.
Fill my heart with
your light, your wisdom,
your joy, your peace.

LIVING THE PRAYER

Today I will urge Christ to come into my day and remain with me. Though Christ never leaves me, why should I still ask him to stay with me? What is the difference between urging, inviting, or merely asking?

THE GOSPEL VISION OF THE PROPHETS

God reveals deep and hidden things;
he knows what is in the darkness,
and light dwells with him.
(Daniel 2:22)

FOLLOWING JESUS WITH JOHN
JESUS, THE DIVINE WORD

We have to consider all the ways that Jesus "speaks" in John's Gospel, as God's very Word in human flesh. Some of those ways aren't verbal; after all, the Gospel tells us that the Word took on our mortal flesh and came to "live among us" and not merely "talk at us." Even though there are many lengthy discourses in John's Gospel in which Jesus speaks more explicitly about who he is (more than in the other Gospels), this is balanced by the importance of the signs that Jesus works. As in all the Gospels, the ultimate sign of God's loving, faithful Word in Jesus is his passion, death, and resurrection. The ongoing sign of the Word living among us is the gift of the Holy Spirit breathed upon the church by the Word.

PRAYER

Breathe on me, Word of God;
fill me with your Spirit
so that I will proclaim your name
and your Good News
in my every thought, word, and deed.

LIVING THE PRAYER

Today I will "speak" God's word non-verbally, in my actions. How can I proclaim the gospel without using words? Do I talk about the deeds my faith leads me to do, or do I just do them in quiet faithfulness?

THE GOSPEL VISION OF THE PROPHETS

For out of Zion shall go forth instruction,
and the word of the LORD from Jerusalem.
(Micah 4:2)

JOHN 1:29

The next day John the Baptist saw Jesus coming toward him and declared, "Here is the Lamb of God who takes away the sin of the world!"

This is a "sneak preview" into the culmination of the work of Jesus. Unlike the other Gospels, Jesus' final meal with his followers in John does not take place on Passover, but the night before, when the Passover lambs were killed. Those unblemished, first-born lambs were a remembrance of the angel of death passing over the children of Israel. As with those lambs, death will not pass over Jesus; his death, however, frees us from sin and eternal death. As we have progressed in discipleship, we have probably discerned events in our lives that later came to fulfillment in our readiness to sacrifice ourselves.

PRAYER

Your will is revealed
in my life, O God.
Let me surrender myself,
always ready to
make the sacrifices
to which you may call me.

LIVING THE PRAYER

Today I will discern how God has led my life, especially in sacrifices I've had to make.
What early events in my life turned out to be God's will?
Which did I think were God's will, but actually were not?

THE GOSPEL VISION OF THE PROPHETS

He was oppressed, and he was afflicted,
     yet he did not open his mouth;
like a lamb that is led to the slaughter,
     and like a sheep that before its shearers is silent,
     so he did not open his mouth.
(Isaiah 53:7)

JOHN 2:16

Jesus told those who were selling the doves, "Take these things out of here! Stop making my Father's house a marketplace!"

"If money is the root of all evil, why do churches want it?" asks a bumper sticker. Religion and money have had a turbulent relationship, across history, cultures, and faith traditions. But it is a mistake to think that money is the root ONLY of evil, or that no good can come from it. Religions have to exist in the world, and one reality of that world is economic. When Jesus cleansed the temple, he was "cleaning house" for his Father: cleaning it of those who would use money for evil, not for blessing. Cleaning it so that its true purpose—prayer and worship, not commerce— could be restored. Like all of God's gifts, it is up to us to use money, and all our resources, for God's desires.

PRAYER

You have blessed me,
most generous God;
help me to be a sign
of your blessing,
using my treasure and talents
as you intend.

LIVING THE PRAYER

Today I will carefully examine how I use money or some other resource that God has given me.
Is there anything I have spent money on that leads me away from God's path? In what ways am I effective in using my resources in the context of my faith?

THE GOSPEL VISION OF THE PROPHETS

For my house shall be called a house of prayer
    for all peoples.
(Isaiah 56:7)

JOHN 3:8

"The wind blows where it chooses, and you hear the sound of it, but you do not know where it comes from or where it goes. So it is with everyone who is born of the Spirit."

Many ancient religions, including Judaism, gave prominent roles to wind and water as signs of divine power on earth. Genesis begins with the spirit/wind moving on the waters. When Jesus teaches Nicodemus about what it means to be truly baptized into him, he uses both the tangible (water) and the intangible (wind). It is only through the power of the Spirit that we can continue to follow Jesus, and that path will always have elusive twists and turns. The Spirit of Jesus, like the wind, calls us to have trust and faith. The best we can do is try to discern its direction and move with it, lest it blow around us, or blow us over.

PRAYER

Spirit who moved
on the waters of my baptism:
continue to move in my life,
and move my heart as well,
making me faithful in discipleship.

LIVING THE PRAYER

Today I will be still for a moment to feel the Spirit move.
Do I sometimes struggle against the direction of the Spirit?
How successful has that struggle been in the past?

THE GOSPEL VISION OF THE PROPHETS

A new heart I will give you, and a new spirit I will put within you. (Ezekiel 36:26)

JOHN 4:28

Then the woman left her water jar and went back to the city.

In the story of Jesus and the woman at the well there are many details to catch our attention: the conflict of Jewish male and Samaritan woman, his knowledge of her sketchy past, his teaching about living waters. The detail that should get more notice is how she left behind her household's water jar to give witness about her encounter with Jesus, source of living water. Drawing water was a crucial, life-or-death activity for a first-century household. By leaving behind her water jar, she is acting like the fishermen who left behind their livelihood to follow Jesus. Today our lives have things that we too must leave behind to do the same, to tell others of our own encounters with Jesus Christ.

PRAYER

What do you want me
to leave behind,
loving, faithful God?
Free me from things that deter me;
let me know the urgency
of proclaiming your word.

LIVING THE PRAYER

Today I will let go of one thing that holds me back as a disciple. How many aspects of my life do I think are crucially important? Are all of them, truly? How might I benefit from being free from at least one of them?

THE GOSPEL VISION OF THE PROPHETS

Then the LORD put out his hand and touched my mouth; and the LORD said to me,
    "Now I have put my words in your mouth."
(Jeremiah 1:9)

"You search the scriptures because you think that in them you have eternal life; and it is they that testify on my behalf."

We have to recall that when Jesus uses the term "scriptures" he's talking about his Jewish heritage: the Torah, perhaps the prophets and psalms as well. But the discourse that this comes from (one of the complex passages about his relationship with the Father and the testimony of the world) illustrates a point that his Jewish predecessors would also have maintained: the scriptures—oral or written—do not and cannot, in and of themselves, give us eternal life. It is Jesus, the Word-made-flesh, the Divine Word who transcends the scriptures, who grants eternal life. The scriptures are, in a way, presented here as merely herald messengers of Jesus. Saint Jerome said that to be ignorant of scripture is to be ignorant of Christ; those who would be disciples must turn to them. But the scriptures alone are not enough.

PRAYER

Your Word and your words,
living God, give me life.
You alone are my salvation,
my redemption, my glory.
You alone lead me
to life everlasting.

LIVING THE PRAYER

Today I will recall one way that the Hebrew scriptures have been a witness to Christ for me.
Should I be more familiar with the Hebrew scriptures? In what ways are they more than mere fortunetelling documents about Jesus?

THE GOSPEL VISION OF THE PROPHETS

You have taken up my cause, O Lord,
    you have redeemed my life.
(Lamentations 3:58)

JOHN 6:26

Jesus answered them, "Very truly, I tell you, you are looking for me, not because you saw signs, but because you ate your fill of the loaves."

Jesus is understandably exasperated here. He has just fed the multitude, thwarted their attempt to crown him, gone through a stormy "chase," and is now involved in this testy discussion before his "Bread of Life" discourse. In spite of all this, his ability to see into and know our human nature is as sharp as always. It's a chronic shortcoming of our relationship with Jesus to be in it only for the stuff we get. (This is sometimes called the "prosperity gospel.") It's like loving somebody for the candy we get on Valentine's Day. The signs of generous divine love worked in our lives must serve only to draw us more deeply into true love with Jesus.

PRAYER

How many are the signs
of your love for me, Lord!
How few are the ways
I honestly respond in love.
Show me the true way to you
this day, every day.

LIVING THE PRAYER

Today I will move beyond surface gratitude for God's goodness. Does God's generosity only lead me, selfishly, to want more? Do I show thankfulness by being a sign of God's love?

THE GOSPEL VISION OF THE PROPHETS

You shall eat in plenty and be satisfied,
    and praise the name of the LORD your God,
    who has dealt wondrously with you.
(Joel 2:26)

JOHN 7:42

"Has not the scripture said that the Messiah is descended from David and comes from Bethlehem, the village where David lived?"

It's not surprising that this problematic scene appears in no Sunday Lectionary Gospel. It casts doubt on Jesus as Messiah by giving his place of birth as Galilee (where Nazareth was), not Bethlehem in Judea. But those who squabbled about Jesus' place of birth miss the point. They are having their arguments in the temple area in Jerusalem, the place of Jesus' destiny. As much as we might enjoy stories of people who come to greatness from lowly origins, we still make the mistake of focusing on their origins (or sometimes our own). We look, as did people in Jesus' day, for some clue or prediction, rather than looking at a person's life to see the work of God, living and active.

PRAYER

Do you really care
where I come from, Lord,
except that I come from you?
You, my Alpha and Omega,
created me, named me,
and you know my destiny.

LIVING THE PRAYER

Today I will call to mind faithful (not necessarily famous) people I admire, who came from lowly places.
What good or great people have influenced me? Was their great work expected of them all along?

THE GOSPEL VISION OF THE PROPHETS

Before I formed you in the womb I knew you,
and before you were born I consecrated you;
I appointed you a prophet to the nations.
(Jeremiah 1:5)

JOHN 8:10

Jesus straightened up and said to her, "Woman, where are they? Has no one condemned you?"

It would have been permissible—in the group ready to stone this woman caught in adultery—for the man with whom she'd been caught to be holding a stone. What would it have been like for her to see his face in that crowd? Even though Roman law had removed the Jewish people's right to perform the death penalty under their religious law, this group of men was still quick to remind her of her fate. She must have felt utterly alone, power-less, unloved, and frightened. In the midst of her fear and their self-righteousness stands Jesus, who simultaneously disperses them and frees her to live rightly, by showing how true love and mercy is more powerful than either her sin or their stones.

PRAYER

Why do I allow my sin
to hold me captive, Lord,
when you show me how
to be free of it?
Let me embrace your merciful love
and live, past my past, in you.

LIVING THE PRAYER

Today I will act as Christ toward someone who has moved beyond a past sin.
Do I still stand ready to condemn others, even when they have moved past a transgression? How often do I chain myself to past sins when God, instead, has forgiven me?

THE GOSPEL VISION OF THE PROPHETS

Do not remember the former things,
or consider the things of old.
(Isaiah 43:18)

JOHN 9:11

The man born blind answered, "The man called Jesus made mud, spread it on my eyes, and said to me, 'Go to Siloam and wash.' Then I went and washed and received my sight."

Try to make mud from dirt just using saliva. It takes a LOT of saliva! The image of Jesus bent over, spitting and spitting in the dirt to make this mud shows us how "down and dirty" divine love will get in order to heal us. Genesis is here, too: it was the breath of the divine mouth and the stuff of earth that first created human beings, and here the mouth of the divine Word in flesh combines with earth again to restore. This healing gave the blind man both sight and courage—the courage to risk being cast out of his community to proclaim God's glory.

PRAYER

When my life is plunged
into darkness, Lord,
help me remember that you, too,
will plunge into that darkness
to rescue me, save me,
make me whole once again.

LIVING THE PRAYER

Today I will tell someone of a healing that God worked in my life. When God helps me overcome troubles, do I keep my gratitude between me and God? Am I willing to share it out loud?

THE GOSPEL VISION OF THE PROPHETS

Your own eyes shall see this, and you shall say, "Great is the LORD beyond the borders of Israel!"
(Malachi 1:5)

And many believed in him there.

It's no surprise that the evangelists prefer to record successes. John caps another set of contentious scenes in the Jerusalem temple with this "success" verse. However, we don't read that "everybody" believed in Jesus, only that "many" did. Today we can still confuse faithfulness with success, mistakenly thinking that our faithful discipleship guarantees that we will never fail to bring others to Christ. Or we can be impatient, thinking that lack of immediate success is the same as no success. Or we can be proud, thinking that we have to know all the ways our discipleship has achieved gospel goals. It's difficult to stay faithful while remembering that the Holy Spirit works on a timeline not our own, in ways we don't always know or perceive.

PRAYER

Keep me faithful, O God,
as you are faithful
to your people.
Let me remember that all victory,
seen and unseen,
belongs to you alone.

LIVING THE PRAYER

Today I will give faithful witness to the gospel in a place where it may not achieve anything.
Do I remain silent sometimes, thinking that attempting to be a faithful disciple will be fruitless? Am I ready to accept failures, as the first followers of Jesus did?

THE GOSPEL VISION OF THE PROPHETS

Look at the nations, and see!
    Be astonished! Be astounded!
For a work is being done in your days
    that you would not believe if you were told.
(Habakkuk 1:5)

Martha said to him, "Yes, Lord, I believe that you are the Messiah, the Son of God, the one coming into the world."

Much is made of Peter professing his belief in Jesus as Messiah (God's anointed) at Caesarea-Philippi in Matthew/Mark/Luke. In John, Martha makes the same profession, without a parallel fuss. In a way, her profession is more difficult: her brother Lazarus has died, and she makes her proclamation before Jesus raises him from the dead. The scene has a number of double meanings going on as well: Jesus stands at a scene of death while he is already in the midst of confrontations that will lead to his own death. Messiahs may be anointed, but so are corpses. Martha's witness reminds us of the life that conquers death, and this life will lead Jesus from being the myrrh-anointed deceased to being God's Son, anointed Messiah.

PRAYER

Living God,
all resurrection and life
come from you.
Help me to believe
and proclaim this every day.

LIVING THE PRAYER

Today I will bring the resurrection and life to someone I know who needs them.
Am I able to see past the death in the world or my own life?
How can I make this known, rather than keeping it to myself?

THE GOSPEL VISION OF THE PROPHETS

The LORD's anointed, the breath of our life,
    was taken in their pits—
the one of whom we said, "Under his shadow
    we shall live among the nations."
(Lamentations 4:20)

JOHN 12:44

Then Jesus cried aloud: "Whoever believes in me believes not in me but in him who sent me."

All of the "I Am" sayings of Jesus are found in John's Gospel (I am the Light of the World, I am the Good Shepherd . . .), but it is a mistake to think that this is because Jesus likes to talk about himself. In this concluding moment of his public ministry, before he faces his passion, death, and resurrection, Jesus reinforces the point that it's not about him; it's about the God whose very Word in flesh he is. The point is made dramatically: Jesus didn't merely speak, but he "cried aloud" this message. When we give witness to the presence of God in the world, we must remember these two things: it is never about us, and—even if not measured in decibels—it must always be loud and clear.

PRAYER

I am your messenger,
loving, living God!
May your message
be heard and seen clearly
in my daily living.
Let me, like your Son Jesus,
lead others to you.

LIVING THE PRAYER

Today I will explicitly point someone away from me and toward God. Am I transparent or translucent in my witness to God's presence in the world? Can an authentic herald of the Good News be other than transparent?

THE GOSPEL VISION OF THE PROPHETS

You are my witnesses, says the LORD,
    and my servant whom I have chosen,
so that you may know and believe me
    and understand that I am he.
(Isaiah 43:10)

JOHN 13:2

The devil had already put it into the heart of Judas son of Simon Iscariot to betray Jesus.

For some in our sophisticated technological world, it is easy to shrug off a personification of evil called the devil, Satan, or any other name. For others it is easy to shrug off personal responsibility for evil in the world or daily living by making the devil the one accountable. Judas already had the devil's plot in his heart when Jesus knelt down to wash his feet. Judas allowed Jesus to touch him, and Jesus humbly served his betrayer as he served the others at table. In spite of the many ways that Jesus had touched Judas' life, there was still an empty place in Judas' heart for evil, an empty place that he hadn't allowed the love of Jesus to fill.

PRAYER

Fill my heart,
my entire being
with your loving kindness,
my God.
Keep me dedicated
to serving others in your name;
keep me far from evil.

LIVING THE PRAYER

Today I will examine my heart for empty places that the devil might occupy.
Do I believe in a personal force who is evil, the way I believe in one who is good? Have I made room in my life for evil in the past?

THE GOSPEL VISION OF THE PROPHETS

Alas for those who devise wickedness
and evil deeds on their beds!
When the morning dawns, they perform it,
because it is in their power.
(Micah 2:1)

JOHN 14:16

"And I will ask the Father, and he will give you another Advocate, to be with you forever."

Advocate, Comforter, Helper, Counselor. As Jesus is saying farewell to those whom he loves before his passion, he promises to ask the Father to send the Spirit, another Advocate for them before the throne of grace. This discourse from John's Gospel is quite tender and touching. Jesus is still most concerned with the well-being (of all kinds) of his followers, even though he is preparing to meet his crucifixion. It is this mysterious, multi-faceted being—the Spirit—who will continue the many ways that Jesus has been the Word of God, the divine presence in their midst. For Jesus too has been their Advocate, Comforter, Helper, and Counselor. That "forever" Advocate was not just for them, but also for us today, and forever.

PRAYER

Stir up your Spirit
in me today, Father;
grant the living presence,
the comfort, the help,
the counsel of Christ
to me today.

LIVING THE PRAYER

Today I will focus on one facet of the Holy Spirit present in my life. Do I truly believe and live in the presence of Christ, still present in the Spirit? Are there new ways I might come to understand the action of the Spirit in my life?

THE GOSPEL VISION OF THE PROPHETS

For I, the LORD your God,
    hold your right hand;
it is I who say to you, "Do not fear,
    I will help you."
(Isaiah 41:13)

"I am giving you these commands so that you may love one another."

Just as it takes a truly classy person to hear the "William Tell Overture" and not think of the Lone Ranger, it takes a person of real spiritual depth to think that we have been given Christ's commands so that we might love one another as the Father loved Christ, and as Christ has loved us. This positive, "right-living" focus is what all divine commands do for us. Sometimes we lose that focus. In selfishness, we think they are guarantees of our redemption if we follow them; in pride, we think that their observance is what makes us better than others. But these sorts of attitudes actually take us away from the commandments' intent: to be God's loving presence in the world.

PRAYER

I love you, Lord;
help me live in your love.
I love you, Lord;
let me follow your commands.
I love you, Lord;
may I strive to love others
as you love us all.

LIVING THE PRAYER

Today I will show God's love toward another person by following a command of Jesus.
Do I follow some of Jesus' commands more than others? Have his commands to love and serve found a place in my life?

THE GOSPEL VISION OF THE PROPHETS

Seek the Lord, all you humble of the land,
    who do his commands;
seek righteousness, seek humility;
    perhaps you may be hidden
    on the day of the Lord's wrath.
(Zephaniah 2:3)

"When a woman is in labor, she has pain, because her hour has come. But when her child is born, she no longer remembers the anguish because of the joy of having brought a human being into the world."

It is fitting that John's Gospel, which is the source of much of the "born again" language of modern Christianity, has Jesus using this illustration of childbirth to describe the experience that the disciples are about to undergo in experiencing his passion, death, and resurrection. It is a pattern in which God's life either supersedes what previously exists—we are born in flesh but must be re-born in water and Spirit—or completely reverses it, as Jesus had just done in the raising of Lazarus, and as will happen soon in his resurrection. The joy of that life transcends all anguish.

PRAYER

When my days are filled
with trials, pain, or anguish,
I call to mind my birth into you,
my joy and help,
my God, my life.

LIVING THE PRAYER

Today I will be God's joyful life for someone in sorrow or anguish. How has God transformed my own times of anguish? Am I willing to be a sign of God's joy?

THE GOSPEL VISION OF THE PROPHETS

Writhe and groan, O daughter Zion,
    like a woman in labor;
for now you shall go forth from the city
    and camp in the open country;
    you shall go to Babylon.
There you shall be rescued,
    there the LORD will redeem you
    from the hands of your enemies.
(Micah 4:10)

JOHN 17:20

"I ask not only on behalf of these, but also on behalf of those who will believe in me through their word."

In the middle of this ecstatic glorification prayer offered immediately before his passion, Jesus puts in this curious nuts-and-bolts bit of information. It's evident that the information isn't for his Father to whom he is praying, but for his followers. On the disciples he places the expectation that others will hear of Jesus—and come to belief—through their own preaching of the kingdom. He likewise cuts off any selfish impulse they might have, thinking that the glory of God soon to be revealed in Jesus' passion, death, and resurrection is only for them. It is also for us, descendants of those who believed in Jesus through the witness of those first followers; it is also for those who will believe through our own word.

PRAYER

I glorify you,
glorious Father of Jesus Christ!
Inspire my heart, guide my tongue
that I may joyfully proclaim
the wonders of your reign
all my days.

LIVING THE PRAYER

Today I will proclaim God's glory as a worthy descendant of Jesus' disciples, a worthy ancestor of disciples to come.
How aware am I of my place on the family tree of faith? What will I hand on to future disciples?

THE GOSPEL VISION OF THE PROPHETS

Who has believed what we have heard?
    And to whom has the arm of the Lord been revealed?
(Isaiah 53:1)

JOHN 18:23

Jesus answered, "If I have spoken wrongly, testify to the wrong. But if I have spoken rightly, why do you strike me?"

Jesus was not the first person in human history to get in trouble for speaking the truth to power. In this scene he defends his teaching in the temple area, a place where the power of religious authority had often turned away from what was right and true. No surprise that Jesus—who identified himself as Way, Truth, and Life—would fearlessly speak the truth in public; no surprise that those in power were not pleased. But even when facing the high priest, Jesus was not able to do anything against the truth, but only for the truth (as Paul would later write to the Corinthians). In the end, it would be on the cross that he would make his ultimate statement of truth.

PRAYER

I sometimes need
your might and courage
to help me speak the truth
that you have placed in my heart.
God of wisdom and truth,
strengthen me, your faithful servant.

LIVING THE PRAYER

Today I will speak the truth in a situation where it may not be easy or popular to do so.
How often have I kept the truth silently to myself? Have I ever tried to silence the truth of the gospel?

THE GOSPEL VISION OF THE PROPHETS

Justice is turned back,
and righteousness stands at a distance;
for truth stumbles in the public square,
and uprightness cannot enter.
(Isaiah 59:14)

And carrying the cross by himself, Jesus went out to what is called The Place of the Skull, which in Hebrew is called Golgotha.

This one verse is the entire "Way of the Cross" from John's Gospel. There is no mention of Simon the Cyrene being compelled to help Jesus, no dialogue with the women of Jerusalem. It is also the first time the word "cross" appears in John. (John's portrait of Jesus does not include the teaching about the cross being the price of discipleship.) John really wants to emphasize the solitary, unique nature of Jesus' sacrificial death on the cross. This example shines for us still: Jesus does not expect anything of us that he was not willing to do himself; his solitary bearing of the cross and sacrifice on Calvary means that none of us will ever have to bear our own cross alone.

PRAYER

How often I feel alone,
abandoned, even by you,
faithful God.
In your Son may I find
my support and example.
Jesus always walks with me.

LIVING THE PRAYER

Today I will share a cross or burden with Jesus.
Am I willing to walk my own way of the cross—even a brief one—as God wills? Do I turn back, thinking I am alone?

THE GOSPEL VISION OF THE PROPHETS

But he was wounded for our transgressions,
    crushed for our iniquities;
upon him was the punishment that made us whole,
    and by his bruises we are healed.
(Isaiah 53:5)

JOHN 20:29

Jesus said to Thomas, "Have you believed because you have seen me? Blessed are those who have not seen and yet have come to believe."

When we think of Beatitudes, we usually think of Matthew's Sermon on the Mount. But any statement from Jesus that begins with "blessed" is a Beatitude. This one describes us today. We have not seen the risen Christ the way his first followers did. Like those first followers we can still be afraid and shaken, as they were after the events of his suffering and death. But he still greets us with "Peace," breathes the Spirit on us in baptism, and names us "blessed" for believing in him. This peace and blessing is not something to be grasped selfishly. They are for our assurance and for our fortification as, in the Spirit, the risen Lord sends us to proclaim the Good News.

PRAYER

When I want proof, my God,
proof that I should have faith,
bring me back to the truth:
Christ, raised from the dead.
Help me to believe.

LIVING THE PRAYER

Today I will believe in what I cannot see.
How strong is my faith when I'm uncertain or afraid? Do I know I am "blessed" in my belief?

THE GOSPEL VISION OF THE PROPHETS

Do not fear, or be afraid;
    have I not told you from of old and declared it?
    You are my witnesses!
Is there any god besides me?
    There is no other rock; I know not one.
(Isaiah 44:8)

But there are also many other things that Jesus did; if every one of them were written down, I suppose that the world itself could not contain the books that would be written.

Testifying and testimony are very important throughout John's Gospel. He writes of the truthfulness of the testimony he has received, and also recounts elsewhere that Jesus did many things not written in the Gospel. There is a completely new twist here, at the very end of the Gospel. John refers to himself in the first person, as "I"—something the evangelists (except for Luke at the very beginning of his Gospel) do not do. But it is through that first person—the "I" that each of us must bring to the gospel—that Jesus continues to work in the world. What other things has Jesus done through everyone who has truly followed him? The world could not contain the record of all those things.

PRAYER

Every day,
loving God,
I will strive to live
in the name of your Son, Jesus.
Through the power
of your Holy Spirit,
may I follow him faithfully.

LIVING THE PRAYER

Today I will do one thing in the name of Jesus, though it will not be written down.
What kinds of commonplace things did Jesus do every day? How might he have filled even those daily events with heavenly grace?

THE GOSPEL VISION OF THE PROPHETS

Bind up the testimony, seal the teaching among my disciples. (Isaiah 8:16)